DYNAMIC PSYCHIATRY
and
THE SENSE OF JUSTICE

DYNAMIC PSYCHIATRY
and
THE SENSE OF JUSTICE

By

WARREN GORMAN, M.D., F.A.C.P.

Consultant in Psychiatry
Formerly Visiting Professor of Psychiatry
College of Law
Lecturer in Nursing
Arizona State University
Tempe, Arizona

WARREN H. GREEN, INC.
St. Louis, Missouri, U.S.A.

Published by

WARREN H. GREEN, INC.
10 South Brentwood Boulevard
Saint Louis, Missouri, U.S.A.

Library of Congress Catalog Card Number 70-96982
ISBN No. 0-87527-106-5

Printed in the United States of America

ACKNOWLEDGEMENTS

Acknowledgement is made of the splendid organization and detailed scholarship by Martin L. Hoffman and D. H. Heath, whose work furnished the basis for extensive development, quotations and paraphrasing in the chapters on the Sense of Justice and Normalcy, respectively. Acknowledgement is also made to the following authors and publishers, for permission to reprint illustrative and stimulating reading material:

David Abrahamsen, M.D., (1965) "The Road to Emotional Maturity" Englewood Cliffs, New Jersey, Prentice-Hall.

The Estates of Edmund Bergler, M.D. and Joost A.M. Meerloo, M.D. (1963) "Justice and Injustice," New York, Grune and Stratton.

Dave Smith and the Los Angeles Times (1968) "The Dark Valley of a Boy's Mind."

The Weekly American (Phoenix, Arizona) for the letters from the son and husband of Mrs. Sellers, on her murder by Robert Benjamin Smith.

W.G.

CONTENTS

DYNAMIC PSYCHIATRY
and
THE SENSE OF JUSTICE

CHAPTER 1

THE DARK VALLEY OF A BOY'S MIND

Dave Smith*

When he was 13, Benny Smith began to experience an identity crisis.

It was not the fashionable sort of identity crises that people discuss over cocktails, nor the sort that moved writers or film directors to create the existential art of the 1960s.

> Inwardly, in one dark valley where his mind comes more and more to dwell, and where no one else can see, corrosive fantasies leap and flicker, finally taking on a life of their own — stronger than that of their quiet, timid creator.
>
> Outwardly, nothing seems changed, except that his remarkable quietness deepens. Benny goes through the motions of an unremarkable adolescence, eating his breakfast, going to school, making good grades, feeling neglected, rarely complaining, reading books, brushing his teeth, going to bed and marking off the humdrum years, five years, as quietly as the soft, inexorable tick of a time-bomb.

On Nov. 12, 1966, Robert Benjamin Smith, now 18, stepped into the Rose-Mar College of Beauty in the quiet Mormon town of Mesa, Ariz. It was a sunny Saturday morning, a time when girls and women flock in for the $1.50 cut-rate for a shampoo and set, so they'll look pretty for Saturday night out.

Already there, just minutes after opening, were three young

3

beauty operators and two young customers, one with her two little daughters.

The youth ordered all seven to lie on the floor, face down, in a circle like wagon-wheel spokes, with their feet pointing out.

Then, laughing and stepping nimbly around the circle between the prone forms, he shot every one of them — trying, but not always succeeding, to get them in the back of the head. Five died.

On Oct. 13, 1967, Benny was ruled mentally competent to stand trial, and on Oct. 24 a seven-woman, five-man jury convicted him of five counts of first-degree murder. On Nov. 8, Superior Judge Laurance T. Wren sentenced him to die, by lethal gas, on Feb. 2, 1968.

The end? No. Benny is still alive, in Death Row at Arizona State Prison at Florence.

But even his death would not end the story. A mother, father and a little sister still love Benny. And somebody loved his victims, too. Questions will haunt these people as long as they live, and will also plague society for as long as it must fear what Benny represents.

His parents, Robert L. Smith and Jessie Trimble, both were born and reared in the south-central Missouri town of Houston (pop. 2,500) seat of Chickasaw County in the gentle Ozark Mountains.

Bob's mother died when he was a year old, his father when he was 13, and then he lived with two aunts. He joined the Air Force in 1939, when he was 18, and after the war he lived in Kansas City, but after a while he went back to Houston.

Jessie was the youngest of three children. Her parents, in their mid-30s when she came along, lived on a farm outside town, and of them she now recalls, "They were always hard-working. You know how farmers are — up bright and early and off to bed early. What I remember was they were always busy, always doing something."

Years later, she also told a neighbor, "My mother used to shout at us when I was a little girl, and I hated it." But was it mostly a happy home? "Well," Jessie says today, "I guess you would say that."

Jessie grew to be strikingly pretty — huge dark eyes in a cameo face, slim as an elf — and still is. And an elfin humor sometimes bubbled unexpectedly from under a placid surface, in those days.

Bob and Jessie started going together after Bob moved back to Houston, and in December, 1946, they were married. A little more than a year later, on Feb. 10, 1948, they had a son. They named him Robert Benjamin, but soon, to avoid the confusion of having two Bobs or Roberts in the house, they were calling him Benny.

Benny's was a difficult birth. Jessie was in labor for 23 hours and heavily sedated. When Benny finally made his delayed appearance he was put in an incubator. And then, strangely: Jessie doesn't remember if she held Benny very much as an infant and she can't remember if she enjoyed it. And did Benny feel loved, as a small child? Jessie is silent for a long moment; then her answer is vague and somehow touching in its honesty: "Well, I think he did . . . to a certain extent."

She does recall that Benny seemed a very passive, quiet baby, except that he cried a lot at night. Mentally, he appeared bright, and began talking at about 10 months, but he was slow in physical development, not sitting until about 8 months nor walking until 18 months. He looked a lot like Jessie; he later grew so handsome he was almost pretty.

Bob, meanwhile was working in the mechanical plant of Houston's weekly newspaper, owned by his sister's husband. Life hummed along peaceably until 1951, when the Korean War began, and Bob, now a major in the Air Force Reserves, was recalled to active duty. Though Bob traveled a lot with the Air Force back during the war, he was never sent to Korea after he was recalled. He spent the next five years close to home.

> Benny started school at 6 and promptly hated it. He tried persistently to miss the bus, and one day Jessie heard him phoning the school to report, "I've chickened out today." Despite an interest in reading, he did poorly. Jessie now recalls, "For the first two or three years, I don't recall his ever saying whether he did or didn't like his teachers. If he disliked them, he hid it around me."

Jessie says she was not then aware that Benny had already learned, at 6, to conceal his feelings but she adds, "Looking back, I'm sure he must not have expressed how he felt about school and things like that."

She also recalls that in his first years of school, "I always thought of him as shy and rather bashful — not extremely but not rough or rowdy like boys usually are." Bob adds, "He was always a very quiet little boy."

In 1956, when Benny was 8, the Air Force sent Bob to Iceland for a year — the only time the family was split during Bob's service career.

During this year, Jessie says, she and Benny went to the movies and swimming a lot and were "real close — maybe closer than most mothers and sons."

A psychoanalyst who later talked to the family got the impression that Jessie "was quite affectionate, perhaps overly affectionate to the boy at this time — and then suddenly cut it off," chiefly because Bob, on his return, feared that the quiet, bookish Benny was becoming "too much of a mamma's boy."

And it was about this time that Benny first gave any outward sign that he was in trouble.

The family had just moved away from Houston and Benny was behind the class in his new school. Although he was obviously bright, he still hated school, did poorly and had to repeat the third grade. Jessie thinks it was mostly because of his sloppy handwriting, which by itself seems a slim reason. Benny's memory is less clear; he later thought it was the fifth grade he repeated.

> But a school advisor noticed that something was wrong with Benny. His physical coordination was still poor. He couldn't tie his shoes or ride a bicycle until he was 9. He was awkward in games and sports, and this retarded friendships with the rough-and-tumble boys his age. He began to feel left out, and responded by withdrawing into a world of daydreams, books and heroes — Caesar, Napoleon, Hannibal.
>
> That school official advised the Smiths to take Benny to a psychiatrist. Bob, just back from Iceland, was jarred by the advice but reassured by Benny's own precocious answer: "I'll solve my problems by myself."

The Smiths fell for it; so did the adviser, who told Benny, "Well that's always the best way." Bob speaks of this now with a sad smile, shaking his head at how different things might have been "if only we hadn't believed him. We thought that was such a smart thing for the little guy to say."

Life rocked along as before, Benny reading in his room, keeping his thoughts to himself, a quiet boy in a quiet house.

And the family moved, from air base to air base – Illinois, Alabama, Colorado, Virginia, Maryland – 10 moves in as many years. It was hard for Benny to make friends, and with so many moves, impossible to keep them.

> "I'm sure all this moving around was very hard on him," Jessie says. Bob adds, "he'd always say that every school he left was the best school he's ever attended and he didn't want to leave it."
>
> But Benny never complained much. There was a rule in the Smith home that one never raised his voice in anger. Jessie, who had hated being shouted at by her mother, adhered to the rule: Bob, who had made the rule, admits he was always first to violate it. But Benny never did. Instead, when he was younger, he would go to his quiet room and cry alone.

For the first time since starting school, Benny had a man teacher in sixth grade and began to like it better. "That was around the time of Kennedy's election," Jessie says, "and he brought home posters and had them pasted all over the windows. He was really for John Kennedy. He was Benny's hero."

It was this year when Benny was 12, that Jessie told him she was going to have a baby. "I guess it came as a little bit of a shock to him," Jessie recalls, "and I remember he cried about it. He went to his room and cried a while. But then he seemed to recover and seemed to be pleased with the idea."

Benny himself, asked about his reaction to Lisa's birth, says, "I can't recall any feelings either way." As to the general mood around home, he says, "I didn't see any improvement."

Lisa was born Nov. 5, 1960, and Jessie laughs a little now when she thinks of the day Benny came home from school and found her and the baby home from the hospital. "He put his arms around me and said, 'Oh, you look just like you always did.' Then he went in to see his baby sister. He wasn't very impressed with her, though. He thought she was kind of ugly."

> Then his grandmother Trimble, whom Benny loves very much, dies of cancer. He is almost getting used to losing his friends by moving, but now here is another loss, somehow worse than the others. It is the first time death has been near Benny; it frightens him terribly.
>
> Benny is 13, just entering puberty, and disturbing things are happening to his body. His father hasn't told him about this, and Benny has no close friends to confide his worries in, so he has no

chance to ask questions or learn from the schoolboy jokes and adolescent exhibitionism common at that age. Always excluded, he has no way of knowing that other boys are airing — and outgrowing — the same fears among themselves. He thinks he is the only person this has ever happened to, and it makes him feel different and alone.

But even more frightening are the pictures in his mind when he masturbates — terrifying fantasies. Women are shooting him, stabbing him . . . old women, girls from school, even his mother — with guns and knives after him . . . He's so afraid . . . He wishes he were dead, and begins to think of doing away with himself.

There is another reason Benny thinks seriously about suicide, now, at 13. He knows that the kids at school can tell what he's thinking, in his masturbation fantasies. He doesn't know how they can tell, but when he sees a group of kids talking and joking together, even when he's too far away to hear, he can sense that they're talking about him, calling him a sissy because he's bookish and poor at sports, saying he's effeminate . . . and worse things . . .

Then the family moved again, in 1962, to a Baltimore suburb, Glen Burnie. From the time they arrived in Glen Burnie, Bob recalls, "he just seemed to cut off all his friendships. Until then he'd had one or two friends, but from then on I don't think he ever had a friend in our home."

But Benny has a good reason for not making friends here. To his horror, he realizes that the kids already know about his fantasies, too. Almost as soon as he starts school he sees the little knots of students at street corners, looking his way and laughing. He knows what they're talking about: him and his shameful thoughts. More and more he thinks of suicide.

In November, 1963, something happened that changed history, and while the United States turned one corner, Benny turned another. John Kennedy, his hero, was murdered.

Benny asked his father to take him to the funeral — only a few miles away — but Bob pointed out that crowds were terrific, it would take hours to get in, and the traffic . . .

Benny agreed, and as Bob recalls now, "He didn't make a huge issue out of it." Bob took him to a service at a convenient air base chapel.

Benny began collecting articles, pictures and books about the assassination, and Bob recalls, "His explanation was that this was going to be of great value to him someday."

What they didn't know then was that Benny had also started collecting material on Lee Harvey Oswald. "I didn't know until I examined it much later that he had as much on Oswald as he did on John Kennedy." Jessie adds, "It seems that Oswald suddenly became a hero to him instead."

Benny copied Oswald's photograph from newspapers with his own camera and searched out articles about him. Later he bought a book on historic assassinations. Then, books on other assassins.

> Suddenly, Benny's heroes are no longer men like Caesar, Lincoln, or Mr. Kennedy, struck down at the height of their fame, but the men who struck them down — Brutus, Booth, Oswald. He becomes fascinated with Germany's role in wars, buys books on Nazism and Hitler, reads "Mein Kampf." A particular hero is World War I aerial combat ace Baron Manfred von Richthoven, who downed 80 Allied planes before he himself was shot down. Benny has a picture of the Baron by his bed.
>
> And other shifts in Benny's attention date from about this time. He doesn't think so much about suicide now, and a strange thing happens in his masturbation fantasies. Instead of women attacking him, he now sees dead and dying women. He has turned the tables on them! He has the upper hand! He feels stronger, somehow, as if he is attaining a kind of power over people, power they don't recognize yet, but will one day.

In 1965, Bob resigned from the Air Force and the family moved West. But first there was Benny's dog — he'd had her 12 years — to be put to sleep. She was too old, couldn't stand the trip, it had to be. "There was his customary matter-of-factness about it," the psychoanalyst said later, "apparently with no understanding of how he felt, no chance for him to say."

Jessie later told the analyst that they moved because Benny wanted to, but when the analyst asked her why he wanted to, it developed that nobody had ever asked him why, really; they just went. They looked over Albuquerque, decided against it and drove on to Arizona.

Mesa is a town of 50,000 and about half its people are members of the Church of Jesus Christ of Latter-day Saints, their lives centered on the sparkling marble Mormon temple that is Mesa's dominant feature.

In such a close-knit religious community, the Smiths, Protestant but not demonstratively religious, were able to settle without being drawn into social alliances that would make them uncomfortable. They were quiet and reserved; privacy was a long habit with them all.

The longest conversation their closest neighbor ever had with Benny was after Jessie and Benny had read Truman Capote's *In Cold Blood* and Genevieve borrowed it. "When I finished it," she recalls, "I saw Benny in the yard one day and he wanted to know what I thought of the psychological picture Capote had drawn of the two killers. We didn't talk long, just a few minutes, but that was the most animated he ever got in conversation with me."

> But again, Benny has a reason for keeping to himself. Once again, just as in Glen Burnie, he discovers that knowledge of his innermost thoughts, his sexual fantasies, is already all over town, almost as if word got there before him. Here it is again, and he can never, never escape the groups of boys who turn and look his way, talking about how odd he is, and the girls suddenly getting quiet as he goes by, knowing among themselves the hideous things he does to them in his sexual make-believe.

Bob and Jessie were under the impression that Benny adjusted to the Arizona move better than others. By this time, his school subjects were a real intellectual challenge and Benny was clearly a superior student, easily in the top third of his class.

But Bob felt he was too quiet and worried about his total disinterest in normal teen-age activities. Finally, Bob and Jessie prevailed upon Benny to join the Mesa High dramatics club because he had become an avid reader of plays. Despite his obsession for privacy, Benny was able to enter this world of extroverts and show-offs. It was, after all, make-believe.

Benny got the juvenile lead in the school play, *You Can't Take It With You,* but when it was performed he insisted that Bob and Jessie not come to see it.

> But toward the end of the school year, he finally had his first date. It was a disaster.
> He had gone to a basketball game with a friend, Bill, and Bill's girl, and at the game they picked up another girl for a foursome. "It seemed as if Bill pressured me into it," Benny later told an analyst. He said the girl was heavily made up and had her hair elaborately teased, and that as they rode around in Bill's back seat, she seemed to be expecting something from him. He didn't know what to do, and vowed he would never date again.

The analyst later wondered if the girl's appearance might have influenced Benny's choice of women in a beauty salon as his victims.

At the end of the year, Benny was elected to next year's senior council — not, as classmates said later, because he was popular but because they felt they should have a studious type in student government.

Then, summer, 1966. As always, Benny spent his time reading, mostly histories of the mighty nations and their wars. But he also began reading Freud and buying books on abnormal psychology, explaining this new interest by telling Jessie he might study it in college. Today Jessie says, "After this all happened, I've come to the conclusion that he probably thought he had a problem and that was why he had those books. I think he was smart enough that he knew he had a problem. Evidently he felt like he couldn't talk to us about it but he was trying to interpret his own illness."

Benny saw one friend a few times that summer — John Towne, who came to Benny's house to play chess and listen to records. Later on, John and Benny planned a five-day trip to Southern California — the first such venture Benny ever planned. Bob was enthusiastic about this evidence of independence, but Jessie was apprehensive. "I wasn't for it," she says, "because I didn't know the boy he was going with very well."

The boys went to San Diego, down to Tijuana, up to Los Angeles, but came home earlier than expected. And then John Towne abruptly severed the friendship. Why he did this and what happened on that trip has never come out, but it had a serious effect on Benny; he won't discuss it today.

Suddenly Benny became irritable and unpredictable — so unusual for him that his parents worried.

"Sometimes the littlest thing would bring on a flareup," says Jessie. "And he got so nervous and tense. He had a little rubber ball and he'd walk up and down the room, just bouncing this ball furiously just like a spring wound up and ready to break."

Bob thought Benny might be having a slight nervous breakdown, possibly from the strain of studying, but though he and Jessie worried, they were not quite moved to act. Benny was a smart, well-behaved youngster, and after all, this was the boy who settled his problems by himself. They hoped that whatever was bothering him would straighten out with time.

> But time is Benny's enemy, and time is gaining on him. For most of his life he has really lived in a secret world he has built in his own mind and merely existed quietly in neglected spaces in the real world. He knows how to maintain and conceal these dual lives, one feeding the other, through the framework of the school routine, and as long as the routine doesn't vary, he can keep both systems going, slipping undetected from the outer world to the inner one.
>
> But now frightening changes loom ahead, threatening to shatter his system. He can't decide what to do after his senior year. College? He has said he might teach, but he doesn't really want to. The Army? Vietnam? He can't go into the Army, because there you're nobody, just one of the crowd. He finally stands out a little because of his academic success, and he can't bear to lose this standing now.
>
> Besides, whatever he does, wherever he goes, he knows there will always be the groups of people talking and staring at him, knowing his thoughts. He can never escape that. It will never be better. He'll be a nothing all his life, after this year, unless he does something — soon — to be somebody.
>
> In that strange valley of the mind that is now his fortress, dark forms move, shapes change, and fantasies wreathe like smoke, one replacing another, until one emerges, stronger than the others. It is a compelling fantasy, and as weeks go by it exerts a growing power over Benny. The fantasies were supposed to be his refuge, his escape; now they frighten him. He feels them growing stronger, himself weaker, almost consumed, unreal. Who is he now? The fantasy wants something from him. Something awful. He must do something, fast. He must do something definite, striking, something that will make him real again. But which is real . . . ? This thing he must do — is it his own idea? Will it break the fantasy's power over him? Or is it really the fantasy's idea, not his, but planted in his mind? So confusing . . . whichever it is . . . peculiar . . . the idea comes out the same . . .
>
> The fantasy commands, and Benny tries to defy it, and the word is the same: kill.

Benny's English class was a small one — 10 girls and four boys who, under Evelyn Denton's guidance, read and discussed philosophical ideas, mostly related to man's inner drives and the acts resulting from them. The class studied Sartre's *No Exit* and other existentialist works, and Mrs. Denton recalls that Benny was fond of Hemingway (a superman who killed himself) and the character of Shakespeare's *Hamlet* (who approached madness before achieving the will to act). She didn't know — and shivered when she learned — that Benny also read Dostoevsky's *Crime and Punishment* and identified strongly with its murderer anti-hero, Raskolnikov.

On the school activity calendar Benny carried in his looseleaf notebook, he had written this reminder to himself under Friday, Nov. 11: "Slaughter on a Saturday." And through the square for the next day he had drawn a large black X.

On the night of Friday, Nov. 11, Benny helped Lisa write her annual letter to Santa Claus. Then he told his folks he had to go to school early next morning to help build a float for the Thanksgiving Day Football game. Before going to bed, he wrote a list of things to remember the next morning and filled a paper sack with things he would need — plastic bags, parachute cord, a mask, tape, rubber gloves, knives and extra ammunition for his 22-caliber revolver.

He arrived at Rose-Mar College of Beauty just as Bonita Sue Canteloupe, 18, a student operator was coming to work. Already there were two other student operators, Glenda Carter, 18, and Mrs. Carol Farmer, 19, and one customer, Mrs. Joyce Sellers, 27, with her small daughters, Debra, 3, and Tamera Lynn, 3 months.

Benny was irritated that the women paid no attention to him, so he fired one shot in the air and ordered them to step into a back room and lie down. One woman asked if he was kidding, so he pointed the gun at Mrs. Canteloupe's head and said, "Do you think I am?" They did as they were told.

The sudden quiet frightened Tamera Lynn and she began to cry. That made Benny angry; he hadn't expected any children to be there, and the crying disrupted the quiet orderly slaughter he had hoped for. He had planned to tie up the women, gag them with tape, and smother them with the plastic bags or maybe strangle them. Now he'd have to hurry and use the gun.

Mary Olsen, frightened now, began to pray. "What's she doing?" snapped Benny, and Mrs. Farmer answered sarcastically, "She's praying, if you don't mind."

"I do," said Benny, so he shot Miss Olsen first.

Perhaps because of his irritation, Benny's marksmanship was off a bit. It took three bullets to kill Mary Olsen and two for Glenda

Carter, who didn't die right away but kept moaning while he attended to the others.

Little Debra Sellers was fatally wounded by a shot in the head, but she kept twitching so he nicked her with a knife and she lay still.

Tamera Lynn's cries grew to screams as she was shot in the arm but her screams were suddenly muffled — and her life was saved — when her mother's body rolled on top of her. Both Joyce Sellers and Carol Farmer were killed by single shots to the head.

Mrs. Canteloupe was shot in the arm and head, but only superficially. "I played dead," she said later. "I kept lying there and I was hoping I would faint or something, but I didn't."

So she heard Benny through it all, laughing as his exhilaration mounted, explaining that nobody cared for him, that he had to kill the little girls because "they'll grow up too. . ."

Mrs. Evelyn Cummings, director of the school, was in a rear office when she heard sharp, cracking noises. Benny was so absorbed in his task that he didn't see her in the doorway or notice as she fled to phone police. Having shot everyone in that room, he reloaded his gun and was wondering whether to check other rooms when the police arrived.

Benny was smiling and amiable as the thunderstruck, smalltown police took in the carnage, and he chided them archly: "You were kind of silly. I could have shot you all at any time."

He burst out laughing as they led him away, smiled brightly at news cameras, and then, in a swift change of mood, thumbed his nose and held his hands to show off the handcuffs.

And he talked and talked. Told of his constitutional rights not to say anything self-incriminating, he talked anyway: he had planned the murders for three months. Once he thought of going back to Houston to kill people in a bank; then he thought of a girls' dormitory; then of a beauty parlor. Richard Speck's murder of eight student nurses in Chicago and Charles Whitman's sniper slaying of 15 in Austin had inspired him. He'd read everything he could about those cases . . .

He didn't think any little children would be involved, but he had sort of hoped for more women — about 10 or 12, say. If his own mother or sister had walked in during the killings, "I would have killed them, too." And why did he do it? "I wanted to get known . . . get myself a name . . . to see the headlines with my name in them before I die."

Phoenix attorney Rod Wood, driving to Benny's arraignment three hours after the murders, was sickened by the crime — particularly the shooting of the children. Wood is just 31, and the biggest fear, he says, was, "What the hell could I say to anybody who'd done such a repellent thing? I knew our whole relationship depended on the first words exchanged, but I didn't know what to say to him."

Later, meeting Benny privately for the first time, Wood noted that Benny seemed perfectly composed, quiet, just waiting for him to speak. They eyed each other warily for a long moment. "Well," drawled Wood, "what have you been doing for excitement lately?" That broke the ice; Benny grinned and began pouring out his story.

Wood saw an insanity plea as the only resort, and so a battery of doctors — six in all — began examining Benny in his cell in Maricopa County Jail. Without exception they diagnosed him as suffering from "schizophrenic reaction, paranoid type."

To Phoenix psychiatrist Otto Bendheim, Benny was "totally devoid of any human emotion — without conscience, feeling, remorse, regret" who admitted he probably would kill again if he ever could. Bendheim said Benny was "the classic picture of schizophrenia" and added: "It is difficult to realize in talking to this man that one is talking to a human being."

Dr. Samuel Wick, former director of Arizona State Mental Hospital, felt that Benny knew the killings were wrong according to the morality of others, but their morality didn't apply to him because he had God-like authority over others — a delusion of grandeur compensating for a deeper sense of inferiority.

> Scottsdale psychoanalyst Kent Durfee said Benny grew up quite indifferent to his parents, particularly his father. "At times he hates him," Durfee said, adding that not long before the murders, after an argument, Benny intended to kill Bob. He had a butcher knife and planned to stab him by surprise if he had entered the room where Benny waited; luckily, Bob didn't happen to come in and Benny cooled off. Bob never even knew of the episode.

In jail, meanwhile Benny found himself in a strange friendship with the prisoner in the next cell, Vernon (Jack) Mahan, 35, five years along on a 20-30 year sentence for his third felony, armed robbery of the Arizona State Treasury.

Mahan had an unusual curiosity about other people's crimes, and another prisoner recalls that Mahan used to send notes, asking them why and how they committed their crimes. The prisoner says Mahan wanted the answers in writing because he claimed the cells were electronically bugged, and he wouldn't want their confessions to be overheard.

Mahan wrote to Benny, he later testified, after first gaining Benny's confidence by suggesting a jailbreak together. He was curious, he said, whether Benny was really insane or only faking.

Benny, wary of most people, answered Mahan's notes and said he was not insane, but that "my attorney is trying to make everyone on the outside think I'm insane." Another time Benny wrote, "You can see how much I trust you, Jack. If the wrong people got hold of this note, they'd really hang me up. Okay, Jack?"

Mahan gave the notes to Chief Criminal Dep. County Atty. Moise Berger.

In March, 1967, Mahan turned state's evidence against his accomplice in the treasury robbery of years back. The accomplice was convicted and Mahan was given out-of-state parole.

> In June, Benny was visited by another psychoanalyst, Dr. Elaine Knutsen, of Sonoma, Calif., who asked him what it meant to kill someone. He said, "To kill is to perform some form of act which stops the body processes — all functions of the body. Then, a blank after that."
>
> Benny explained how, by his reasoning, it was simply time for his victims to be dead and therefore he was not wrong in killing them. "In its own way," says Dr. Knutsen, "his thinking is a perfectly logical syllogism that would go something like this: 'People have a time to die. God decides when. This is God's power. God is not wrong. Therefore in taking God's power I am not wrong!' "

Dr. Knutsen describes Benny's scholarliness as a defense against the crushing depression, fear and hopelessness that swept in on him when he was mentally idle, not riveting his attention on books.

And as to his choice of women as victims, did this mean Benny was homosexual? No, Dr. Knutsen decided, because Benny was able to say without a trace of discomfort that he had no interest in his own sex. By the same token, he admitted, he had never once tried to imagine what sexual relations with a woman might be like, although he didn't think he would like it. At that point in his life, she concluded, "He hadn't really got through the adolescent task of establishing his own sexuality. That's why he relied so much on masturbation and masturbation fantasies. And that's not perversion, that's just delayed development."

> It was with Dr. Knutsen that Benny came close to tears as he discussed his life. Talking of his loneliness, his lack of someone to understand him, she asked if he would like to express his feelings to someone. Benny's eyes glistened, she recalls, "and he said yes, he would like that, and there seemed to be almost a pleading tone to his response."
> This brief glimpse beneath his unemotional exterior convinced her that Benny was treatable — perhaps even curable — "but that," she says today, "was as of last June. By now he may be unreachable."

Benny's trial began Sept. 11. Wood entered a plea of innocent by reason of insanity.

Among the six doctors who examined Benny personally, all agreed that he knew, whether or not he felt, the difference between right and wrong and that he comprehended the charges, intellectually at least.

On Oct. 14, Judge Wren declared: "I find lack of emotion not to be essential to an adequate defense by counsel. Being able to relate facts accurately is of more consequence than emotional involvement. It is the finding of the court that the defendant is fully competent . . ."

Four months later, one of the six doctors, Phoenix psychiatrist Carl Breitner, told a class of psychology students that Benny "had a motive we cannot readily understand." He said Benny was mentally ill, but not sufficiently to be found insane under present Arizona law. "Insane he may be in laymen's terms," said Breitner, "but not under the law."

The turning point in Benny's trial came on Oct. 21, three days before the end, when prosecuting attorney Berger produced Jack Mahan and the notes he and Benny had exchanged. Benny had admitted he was feigning insanity, Berger argued, and was trying to fool the jury into acquitting him so he could to to the state hospital instead of the gas chamber.

Wood called Berger to the stand to ask if the county attorney's office had solicited Mahan to get written confidences from Benny; Berger denied it. Mahan said his only motive was curiosity and that he had no deal with Berger, but that he gave the notes to Berger when he came to discuss parole.

Wood said Benny, "like most insane people, refuses to admit he's mentally ill. So to gain his confidence, I told him I knew he was sane, but that it was my job to make everybody think he was insane." Wood then recalled Dr. Wick and Dr. Durfee, who agreed that Benny's claim of sanity and his belief that he could fool the jury were perfectly in keeping with his type of illness.

County Atty. Robert Corbin, in closing argument for the prosecution, reminded the jury that if they found Benny innocent, he would go to a state hospital from which he could easily be released in a few years. Much had been made, he said of Benny's starved emotional life and his mental condition. "It's great to feel sympathy," he said, "but let's not forget the victims, too."

The jury took one hour and 49 minutes to conclude that Benny was sane under the law and therefore guilty. The death penalty was mandatory. Benny heard the verdict without a flicker of emotion, then shrugged and smiled.

As formal sentence was passed, Judge Wren asked Benny, "Do you have anything you wish to say in your behalf?" Benny answered, "No, sir, I do not." Those five words were the only words Benny ever spoke in court. A few minutes later, in a meeting much like their first, Benny and Wood faced each other quietly. "Well," said Wood, "what do you think?" Benny shrugged and smiled again, and said, "Some days are worse than others."

Bob and Jessie drive the 62 miles down to Florence every Saturday to see Benny. They often find him depressed, so the visits are quiet ones and they come away in a somber, despairing mood.

At home they face nearly $400,000 in lawsuits brought by the families of Benny's victims. "There's no point in even thinking about that," says Bob. "I could never earn that much, so I just don't think about it."

What they do think about are the long, painful years ahead.

They are only in their 40s and will have many years to live with the bitterest knowledge a parent can learn. "Sometimes," Jessie wrote Genevieve two months ago, "Bob feels life is hardly worth living, and I must say I see his point."

But most of the time they feel there is something to hang onto. There is Lisa, who, Genevieve says, is getting the show of love, the little pats and hugs, that Benny missed.

Then there is Benny. "People ask if we might ever move away from Mesa," says Bob, "but we won't. The town has been kind to us, and besides, we have to stay. Our boy is here."

> And somehow, since the tragedy, communication between Benny and his parents has deepened a little — not much, but a little. Not long ago he wrote Bob and Jessie:
>
> "There are some things that are easier to say on paper than in person — things that I've wanted to say for a long time. I'm sorry for what I've done to hurt you. You deserve a better son than me — and that's for sure. I love you both very much — always have and always will. And I want you to tell Lisa that I love her, too."

And in another letter: "There's not much to say now except that I love you and think of you often. I always will. Maybe I sound a little stupid, but I'll quote something to you:

> "The moving finger writes; and, having writ
> Moves on: nor all your piety nor wit
> Shall lure it back to cancel half a line
> Nor all your tears wash out a word of it."

There it is — the meager, quiet life of Benny Smith. Is every fact equally relevant to the horrifying young manhood to which he grew?

Maybe not. But these things happened to this lonely, unremarkable boy who did this thing — to make a name for himself.

There was another lonely, unremarkable boy once, who wanted to do something to make a name for himself. He did. His name was Oswald.

"Putting this boy to death is like putting a head of cabbage to death," says Ron Wood. "Executing him will do nothing at all to help us understand why people like him or Oswald or Speck go out and murder perfect strangers.

"We can't just kill these people and try to forget that things like this happen. Instead we should be studying these killers and applying what we learn to public mental health programs, or else crimes like this will be repeated, over and over."

To whatever degree any of us suffers from these senseless deaths, part of our pain grows from the feeling that it was a blind lottery that chose its victims for no apparent reason. The mind picks over and over through illogical but unalterable facts, trying to find a reason, extract a meaning, prove a moral that isn't there. And with no meaning in the death, life itself seems absurd, a mindless joke on us all.

Someday, if someone could understand, a sensitive teacher, neighbor or parent might possibly do just a little extra, say a few words of love and encouragement and perhaps change the course of a lonely 13-year-old who had begun to hate the world.

But if no one ever understands and says those words, . . . He might grow up to spend his hate on women in a beauty shop, or nurses in a dormitory, or students on a campus. He might even kill a President.

*   *   *

Three and a half years after Mrs. Sellers was killed, her son, Dean K. Sellers, and her husband, Robert S. Sellers, wrote these accounts of that event to the *Weekly American.**

The son wrote:

"In November of 1966, I was serving on a full-time mission for the Church of Jesus Christ of Latter-Day Saints. To those who don't understand what a mission is, at the age of 19 a young man has the privilege to serve full time with no pay, in the service of the church.

"I had been gone for about four months from home at the time. My mission president called me into his personal office and told me that morning that three of my family members had been murdered in a beauty salon in Mesa, Arizona. I remember the complete feeling of despair and anger. I felt as though the whole world had fallen out from under me.

"It took everything I had in faith and determination to stay in the mission field. At that point, I knew the only way I could keep

* Reprinted by permission of the *Weekly American*, Phoenix, Arizona.

from continually dwelling on the disaster was to continue my mission and work so hard that I would have little time to dwell on that awful day."

The father wrote:

"We immediately left for the hospital; upon arrival in the emergency room I could see the deep concern on the faces of the doctors and nurses. Up to this time I couldn't believe what was happening; it all seemed like it was a horrible dream. The reality of the situation struck me like a bolt of lightening when I entered a small private room in the emergency room and saw my wife lying lifeless.

"I picked her up and embraced her close to me to see if there was any life left. I remember I was told by a nurse that she had died instantly and would I please come in to the general emergency area to identify a little girl.

"Where was she, where was my baby? They led me to another room nearby and as I approached I could hear a baby crying loudly. I bolted for the door and saw her lying on an operating table, a doctor and nurse performing surgery on her little arm. I began to say, 'No, no, please no God. Enough is enough. Please don't let my baby die, too.' The doctor looked over his shoulder and said that she would be all right.

"At this point, I said a prayer in my heart, thanking my Heavenly Father for saving her life. At this time, my bishop asked to go home with me because he wanted to talk to me. After our talk, I went to my mother's home where all my relatives and close friends came to express their sympathy.

"It seemed like the whole city of Mesa wanted to express their bereavment".

*   *   *

So much for the story of a sick boy and the crime he committed. Smith was sentenced to death and sent to the Arizona State Prison to await this sentence which will never be carried out. While on death row, he was caught by the guards while Smith was attempting to saw off the leg of another inmate with a hacksaw, apparently with his cooperation. After extensive surgery, the leg was saved.

In 1972, Smith voluntarily pled guilty to first degree murder, and after some constitutional debate in the Superior Court, was sentenced to life imprisonment and, in addition, to two consecutive prison terms of 75 to 99 years each.

Now in the next chapter, let us examine the development of the normal personality, with an eye to the development of criminal trends.

CHAPTER 2

DEVELOPMENT OF
A NORMAL PERSONALITY

The normal personality develops as a result of physical factors, social factors and psychologic factors converging on the infant and the child. It is probable that the physical or biological patterns are the most fundamental, even though we know more about the psychological forces which shape the personality than we do about the social or the physical vectors.

But a basic trend in development of the personality, which is fundamentally determined in its broad aspects by biologic energies, and channelled in a general way into social patterns, has to have a distinctive psychological development in an individual for that person to express himself as the personality which he has become.

For this reason we shall examine in some detail the psychic factors which shape the personality, using data from the study of normal individuals as well as those from abnormal psychology and psychiatry. We begin by defining the nature of the structures of the personality — the Id, Ego and Superego, then go on to the compartments of the personality — the Conscious, Preconscious, and Unconscious — in order to discuss more clearly the development of the instinctual drives in preadolescence and adolescence. We then introduce the "Sense of Justice" which will be discussed by a multidisciplinary method in the last chapter.

THE STRUCTURAL THEORY
OF THE PERSONALITY

The structures of the personality are not composed of cells or tissues and are not made of brick and mortar, but are the familiar Id, Ego and Superego. These structures are abstractions that have been given appropriate names for fuller understanding and usage, in order to represent dynamic components of the personality which continually interact with each other and with the environment. Each structure performs functions which are generally the same in all individuals, be they well or ill. But the dynamic transactions among these structures result in the distinctive character of an individual's personality.

Id

> The Id is the structure which generally is equivalent to the *elán vitale* of Bergson. It contains the life drives of the individual, being therefore the repository of the strivings for pleasure and biologic survival. The principal life drive — or libido — is a vital force whose aim is pleasure. Sexuality is one of the many manifestations of the pleasure drive.
>
> The Id makes demands, rather than making negotiations or compromises. Once aroused, it demands full satisfaction, by the all-or-none response. The Id is peremptory, demanding immediate gratification. The striving of the Id for pleasure is the basic rule of the "pleasure principle," differing markedly from the "reality principle" which resides largely in the Ego.

Most of the Id, but not all, is unconscious (Figure A).

Ego

The ego is that structure which conducts transactions with reality and with phenomena on the exterior of the personality, and deals with the other psychic structures on its interior. It is therefore the guardian of the gate that stands between the outer world and the inner psychology of the self. As the content of the world grows and as the content of the self grows, soo, too, does the ego. Much of the growth of the ego is organized by learning.

The Ego is adaptive, interpretive and executive in function,

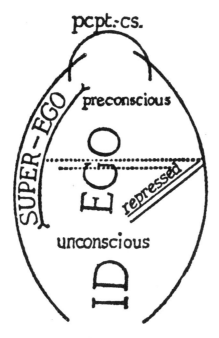

Figure A. Freud's (1933) personality structural diagram.

being responsible for perception, thinking, memory and judgment. Ego strength is the ability of the individual to adapt by means of strengthening himself and/or altering the objective environment.

Most of the Ego is conscious.

The "reality principle" resides largely in the Ego, and results in the individual deferring to his needs in objective reality, rather than to the pleasure demands of his importunate Id.

Superego

The Superego is a controlling body, of which somewhat more resides in the Unconscious than in the Conscious. The Superego modifies the expression by the Ego of those strivings which originate in the Id, being responsible for protection, criticism and punishment. Its two principal components are the Conscience and the Ego-Ideal.

a. The Conscience is a principally conscious portion of the

Superego. The conscience contains the rules of behavior, when those rules are expressed as prohibitions — Thou shall not soil, attack, yearn for incest, etc. The conscience' development is strongly influenced by the cultural environment, so that an individual tends to be imprinted with the societal rules, or *per contra*, with the unruliness, or even the criminality of his childhood background.

b. The Ego-Ideal is principally an unconscious portion of the Superego. This Ego-Ideal contains a distillation of traits which originally were possessed by persons whom the individual loved or feared, such as parents, teachers, conquerors or criminals.

In preparation for the thesis that the development of the superego is defective in the psychopathic criminal, we shall now give some dynamic details of the early formation of the Superego. This development leads to the reward — punishment dichotomy, which is a psychological precursor to penology.

Reward

The Superego originates when the child accepts the feeling from a parent or a parent surrogate, that that which feels "good" such as crude raw pleasures, are really "bad." Primitively, this acceptance has its physical basis in the child being rewarded for the full control of the sphincters of his bladder and of his anus. Later, the child accepts the abstraction in general that what feels good is actually bad, rather than being trained to accept each individual event. (Footnote: This abstraction is well established in the Calvinist moral scheme of the Western world. To emphasize this point, a witty and cynical observer was fond of saying in his lectures, "And out of this lie came morality"! (21).

Punishment and The Lex Talionis

Acceptance of the Lex Talionis (from Latin *talio*, like, as in *retaliare*, to retaliate) is fostered in the child both by reward and by punishment. This is an example of the positive and the negative functioning together in the formation of character. It also is most pertinent to us here because this transgression — punishment system is the psychological prototype of the penal system which our society utilizes.

The anatomy of punishment is psychologically most significant. The child who screams a forbidden phrase may be punished by having his mouth covered, washed out with soap or may receive a slap on the mouth. The child's soiling with feces is punished by spanking the buttocks, or the perianal area. When he or she plays with his genitals, the child's hand is removed or restrained. The child's persistence in this act may evoke retaliation which will consist in being slapped on the offending hand. This is the Lex Talionis — an eye for an eye, a tooth for a tooth — which appears both in psychology and in penology (21).

Reinforcement

The internalizing of moral abstractions such as good and bad, right and wrong, which originate as the "sphincter morality" of the child, are very difficult for a child who is under eight years of age. Repetition and reinforcement, both of the reward and of the punishment, are necessary at this age. Reinforcing punishment can be threatened directly by the parent, or by the parent invoking a threatening figure, such as officers, police, and the "bogeyman." This is the basis of the normal fear of being stopped by authority, or being served a summons.

> In the development of the Superego, the prohibitions or commandments are mainly auditory, as they are given to the child in spoken words. In later normal development, he can even hear the inner "voice of conscience." One reaction to these prohibitions results in the child resisting the words of these prohibitions, which he can generalize to resisting the learning of words, and even to the learning of language.

TOPOGRAPHICAL THEORY OF THE PERSONALITY

Depicting the topographical theory of the personality is best done by a map (Figure B) which shows the Unconscious and the Conscious and Preconscious, with the Unconscious and the Preconscious in the area of unawareness. The Unconscious is by far the larger and weightier portion of the personality.

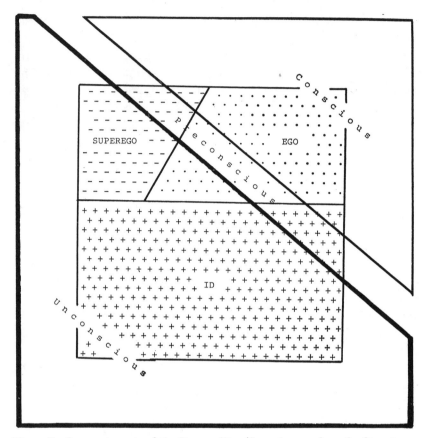

Figure B. Compartments of the Personality. (Superimposed on the Structures of the Personality.)

The Conscious is small, and dynamically far less significant than the Unconscious. The Preconscious is a tiny but traversable pathway between the other topographic zones, being in fact a trail that becomes passable only when the psychological work of overcoming repression is done. This work is performed when we recall lost associations or repressed memories, and in those forms of psychotherapy which require verbal associations.

Such a topographic plan has been likened to an iceberg, of which we readily perceive only that small portion which is above the surface of the water, comparable to the Conscious, while the iceberg's great mass, its rough forms and its jagged edges, lie invisibly below in the Unconscious.

One reason that the Unconscious occupies so great a mass is that it is the repository of all stimuli which have been received during the history of the individual. Were the Conscious, instead of the Unconscious, to retain all the stimuli which fall on any one person, he would seethe with stimulation with his sensory pool in a roil, becoming unable to attend appropriately to the significant features of the present environment. In addition, we have learned that the Unconscious also contains the raw, crude, violent biologic drives of the individual, which appear to be part of his protoplasmic heredity. Since many of these drives are prohibited, and are punishable if they are acted out, or are potentially punishable if they are thought out, they are placed in the Unconscious. (Concerning the relation between the terms "thought out" and "acted out," we recall how Freud wrote that thinking is an experimental form of action.)

Some basic phenomena that depend on the unconscious mind will be described here. They are repression and magic, and the two fundamental varieties of mental reaction — the Primary Process and the Secondary Process.

Repression

Repression is the principal method by which material is relegated to the unconscious, and takes two forms — primary repression and secondary repression. In primary repression, a forbidden or dangerous urge is banished to the Unconscious, immediately on the emergence of that urge, without consciousness of the entire process. In secondary repression, a feeling that had once been conscious is placed in the area of unawareness, by action of forces in the Unconscious. Both forms of repression are performed unconsciously, as opposed to suppression. In suppression, an individual consciously attempts, and may succeed, in making himself unaware of a stimulus.

The preconscious (or the foreconscious) is that area of the personality in which a conscious expenditure of energy will enable unconscious material to become conscious. This energy is often expended by means of encouraging associations to real events, in a permissive setting, which leads to retrieving "forgotten" or repressed behaviors or affects, that had previously been in the

Unconscious. Another method of recovery depends on the fact that dreams are the royal road to the unconscious, which therefore utilizes associations to dreams and their interpretation. This latter method has received brilliant investigative study (24) in the form of formal psychoanalysis.

Magic

We are surrounded by the sea of the Unconscious, for magic, which at bottom is the transmutation of unconscious material into reality, is all around us. We invoke blessings on a sneeze, knock on wood, omit the 13th floor of an apartment building, read the astrology column in a newspaper, and we consult people to advise us concerning our past or future on the basis of our tea leaves, date of birth, or the lines on our palms. We repose faith in persons who remind us of people we like, we like individuals because they recall to us men and women who have loved us, and continually we seek escape from the objective and consciously experienced world by means of fantasies, drugs, and dreams (82).

Primary Process

The unconscious uses a method of discharging tensions which we have seen as a feature of the Id, and which is called the Primary Process. This primary process aims to achieve elementary pleasure, by means of the direct discharge of tensions, without being encumbered by the restrictions of reality, time, order or logical considerations. It is not problem-solving in nature, but is instead a primitive pleasure-seeking approach, which like magic or fantasy, yields only basal satisfactions. It is not logic, but is instead the psychologic concretion of wishes with the emotions, and is a constant theme in our daily living, loving and dying.

Examples of primary process expressions are: "I'll have a good dinner now, and then start dieting on Monday." "I trust him because he has an honest face." A wordless expression is that of the fantasy which precipitates the female orgasm, and a very wordy expression frequently related, is ". . . married, and will live happily thereafter." And here we have some brothy verse by a sturdy Hibernian, Alexander Pope, from his *Essays on Man.*

Alas what wonder; man's superior part
Unchecked may rise, and climb from art to art
But when his own great work is but begun
What reason weaves, by passion is undone.

Secondary Process

Now in the Conscious, we find another process which is the sophisticated but inconstant adversary of the primary process. This adversary, which is called the Secondary Process, is a variety of reasoning rather than a method of emotional discharge, so that it cannot survive in the Unconscious. In Secondary Process reasoning, the individual accepts a delay in gratification and a diminution in short term emotional returns, in order to achieve a greater yield of long term pleasure.

The Secondary Process is a prime ingredient of maturity in the individual. In a society, it is necessary for civilization. But when wrestling with the passions of the primary process it is weak, and frequently undone. Perhaps with this in mind or Alexander Pope's phrase in his memory, an unknown poet scrawled on a university wall:

"Alas!"

Such graffiti can be portraits of reality: Suicide, which is the tenth most common cause of death in the general population, in adolescents is second, following accidents.

THE DEVELOPMENT OF INSTINCTUAL DRIVES

The libido theory postulates that man has an instinctual drive or a striving to gain personal pleasure. This instinctual striving is called the libido. Since sexuality is a significant component of the pleasure drive, sexuality is therefore a significant component of the libido. But there are many other components of the libido in addition to sexuality. These components include touching, tasting, moving, and the functioning of many organ systems, which will be described below. The pleasurable results of these strivings are felt both actively — as in taking pleasure — and also passively — as in being given pleasure, with the active and passive modes of expression being in force at the same time. Thus the lover who holds the hand of his beloved not only stimulates her by his touch, but is also being stimulated.

> The sex drive of the human female deserves emphasis, independent of any theoretic considerations. In comparison with other primates, the sexuality of woman is prodigious. The females of these other big-brained mammals have regular but very short periods of sexual receptivity, they are occupied with pregnancy and infant raising throughout the major portion of their lives, and they show no signs of orgasm. The human female is frequently orgastic, pregnant relatively rarely and is sexually receptive through almost her entire life. From the vantage point of a comparative biologist, the human female is in a perennial state of heat, both physiologically and psychologically.

We can localize the development of the libido to significant body parts. Observations of human growth have shown that various zones of the body play a major role in the individual's pleasurable contact with the environment. Certain of these zones become dominant during four major chronological periods of maturation, which are described as the oral, anal, phallic and latency phases. Despite the dominance of a particular libidinal zone during a particular phase in the individual's development, each zone retains a significant quality of pleasure-giving potential throughout life.

Oral Zone: Birth to 1 1/2 Years.

In the oral phase (more accurately, the intestinal phase), which begins at birth and persists to about the time that the child can walk fairly well, the organs which dominate in the pleasure drive are the mouth, lips, tongue and the gastrointestinal viscera. In addition, but to a lesser extent, pleasurable stimulation is received through the skin in general, the temperature sensors in particular, and the organs of equilibrium. An early and passive phase is oral reflex sucking, and a later and active phase is biting.

In the adult, normal residuals of this phase are the pleasures of eating or kissing. Socially, we "have a drink together," or share bread with a companion (recalling the Latin root *pan* meaning bread.) Some abnormal residuals are bruxism, which is the repetitive clenching of the jaw and grinding of the teeth, or the act of fellatio or cunnilinguous being preferred to the union of the genitals.

"Polymorphous Perverse"

In the oral stage, the child often receives intensive tender attention by the mother and the remainder of the community. If he is wet, mother will dry him; if he appears hungry, he will be given the breast or other feeding; if he utters a sound that resembles the root of a word or a phoneme, he may be praised for talking; and if he soils, few, if any, grumble. Almost no policy of prohibition is applied at this age, for the infant is freely permitted the exercise of almost every one of his abilities. To the infant, it is as if every need and every wish for pleasure were to be fully satisfied, at the moment that the need of the wish should appear, without any possibility of doing wrong.

During this oral stage, the infant may exhibit behaviors which he performs with minimal control by his parent. An adult who would show this style of behavior would be a monster. This in a child is a normal phase which is called the "polymorphous perverse" phase, being so called because the infant's behavior may take any form within his physical capability, and assume any perversity, in his attempt to gain gratification. But this polymorphous perverse activity in an older child or in an adult would be monstrous and uniformly prohibited.

Anal Zone: Age 1 1/2 to 3 Years

In the anal phase, which evolves during the period in which the child is learning to talk, it is the anus, the rectum and the bladder which become the dominant organs. The active pleasures are those of expelling urine and feces, with its concomitant stimulation, while the passive pleasures include retention of these materials. When she is giving toilet training to the child, the parent or parental surrogate interferes with these primitive pleasures. Most significantly, the parent figure introduces mild punishment by verbal disapproval and physical chastisement. Thus punishment is introduced in direct relation to pleasure.

The child's relationship with his training parent can be summarized by this verbal exchange.

Parent: "Instead of my punishing you, do this for me and I will love you for it."

Child: "You're making me give up some pleasure but I'll get some gains."

Here we have the beginnings of mutuality in a relationship. It is also the prototype of a love relationship.

At a quite basal level of behavior, then, the child is deterred by punishment and rewarded by love, for doing something for someone else. This is the forerunner of ego control.

In the adult, normal relics of the anal phase are the retentive phenomena of neatness, thrift and compliance, or the advisory given me by a distinguished jurist, that success on the bench is sometimes dominated by developing a distensible bladder. Anal humor, depending on a sudden blast of a pleasurable surprise, also belongs in this category. On the abnormal side, abnormal adult traits of anal origin are pathologic cleanliness (to overcome soiling) or hoarding. So, too, is excessive sadomasochism, in which an individual figuratively muddies the waters around him, with the unconscious expectation that the results will include difficulties and punishment. A mild form of abnormal sado-masochism is seen in a marriage in which the partners participate in degrading each other and suffering degradation at the other's hands.

Phallic Zone: Age 3-7 Years

In the phallic phase, which takes place during the era of great curiosity, exploration and acquisition of skills, the organ which is dominant is the phallus. In the male the phallus is the penis, and in the female it is the penis's anatomic and physiologic counterpart, the clitoris. While the phallus of either sex is a part of the genitals, this phase is preferably called phallic rather than genital, because of the special psychological use to which the phallus is put.

Boys' Phallic Phase

1. In boys, there are two stages to the phallic period, both described by terms which are symbolic, and not anatomically definitive or associated with any irreversible physical alteration —

masturbation and castration. In the masturbatory phase the boy rediscovers that his penis can be stimulated to erection. This item had been passively discovered early in infancy, when boys have spontaneous erections or in response to stimulation such as cleaning by the nurse. (Recent studies of sleep shows that in infant boys erections take place spontaneously and frequently during sleep.) However, in the phallic development the boy himself stimulates his penis to producing erection. (True ejaculation is not possible until puberty, and since completed male masturbation requires ejaculation, the term masturbation is symbolic.)

Simultaneous with this masturbatory activity is the association, in fantasy, of the nurse, mother or another female figure. Interfering most severely with it in fantasy is the presence of the male figure or father. This is, of course, the familiar Oedipus rivalry, in which the boy fantasies the dispatch of his male rival, in order to win the full possession of a female.

2. But a second stage then appears, this being the stage of symbolic castration. In his explorations, the boy realizes that the female does not have a penis. With his straightforward youthful reasoning, he assumes that she once did have this organ, but that it had been removed. Exercising the simplicity of the Lex Talionis — an eye for an eye, a tooth for a tooth — he assumes that the female was castrated of her penis. The crime, he assumes, was one of masturbatory fantasy or behavior.

With this danger in his mind's eye, the boy foregoes the physical stimulation of his phallus, with its psychical concomitants. He then takes satisfaction in identifying with a male figure who is mature, such as a father image. This father image or other male image is given the psychological authority to act out in real life the drama of the little boys' fantasy.

Thus we obtain as normal residuals of this phallic stage in the male such features as the development of physical and mental strength, or of pride in potency. Mild abnormalities which derive from this phase are excessive exhibition of potency, or guilt over sexual impotence.

Girls' Phallic Phase

The female evolution through the phallic phase, which takes place during the same ages as the males', also has two stages, although it is less incisively indicated by human anatomy. In this development, the girl realizes that a boy has a penis, but that she does not. Worse than that, self stimulation of her clitoris produces no ostensible result which is grossly comparable to the appearance of an erect penis, or even a flaccid one.

For this defect, she blames her mother, who is female, too, and who gave birth to her, so that she then renounces her mother. For relief, she then turns to a father image, with the fantasy that he will give her a penis. This fantasy is supported by a parallel fantasy that he will give her a baby, just as he had given one to mother, if she will be receptive to father. The physical symbolization of this receptiveness cannot be accomplished through the clitoris, which is a solid organ. But it can be performed by means of the vagina, which has an opening to the exterior of the body, and contains a cavity of potential size so great that it can contain a baby.

Normal adult relics of the early female phallic period include attention to grooming, to skin and hair and beauty, for a certain amount of subjective enjoyment. Abnormal relics include hysterical conversion symptoms, in which she focusses on her bodily feelings to the exclusion of the feelings of significant other persons.

Latency Phase: Age 7-12

The latency phase follows the phallic, or Oedipal phase and usually terminates with adolescence. It is called latency because of the temporary diminution in manifest sexual interest that takes place during this time. But while sexual interest is latent, there are enormous strides in general physical and intellectual adaptation. In addition, the child learns to manage aggressive impulses, enters into gang and group formation, and develops a set of values, which determine his feeling of good and bad, right or wrong. During the latency period, no single zone of the body is predominant in the process of striving for pleasure.

These maturations of the boy and the girl may be summarized by saying that during the phase of latency, there are two major developments:

1. The resolution of the Oedipus Complex.
2. The development of a cohesive Superego.

which can both be explained by Freud's statement that the "Superego is the heir of the Oedipus Complex."

As the pre-teen age youngster resolves the Oedipus Complex, he learns that the crime of his or her fantasy has been shared by his peers. Instead of committing the Oedipal crime, then to receive its talion castigation, he develops a system of psychical penology that is far more broad in its scope, but less swift and less sure in the provisions of its punishment. He develops a code of morality, in which transgression does not consist centrally of the incestual sin, but of all forms of wrongdoing. He develops a system of punishment which emphasizes the psychical penalty over the physical, being gentler by far than the fury of his Oedipal retribution.

The Individual's Sense of Guilt

But through his socialization, the individual in his formative years goes beyond the triangular Oedipal situation with its cast of three actors. First having internalized the concept of corporeal punishment, and the abstraction of prohibition, he develops an individual sense of guilt. This sense of guilt was originally derived from outside influences, but after it has been formed, becomes an organ of the personality. It is as if the growing child would say, "He would kill me for this," but later, with the development of his superego, feels "It is wrong in my mind."

Secondly, having formed an individual sense of guilt, he strengthens this new organic portion of his personality by using it, not only within the microcommunity which is composed of his own family, but within the community at large, or the society of which he is a unit. It is as if he were to say, "It is wrong in my mind, just as it is in everyone's." Thus, we see the emergence of the sense of guilt as a social limb of the Superego (3).

Sense of Guilt in Society

Yet the sense of guilt also generates rewards. A universal code frees the individual from the immediacy of being punished or of dealing summary punishment to others. At the same time, it permits him to participate in the administration of punishment in an impersonal fashion, when his society performs its punishing duties. Thus he may read of a death penalty while being insulated by his social construct from the starkness of the execution.

But other positive values are to be had by the Superego's inheritance of the Oedipus Complex. It is the acquisition of a sense of justice. The sharing of this sense of justice provides a reality-oriented affectual contact with one's peers. This social relationship, whose formation is based on the group having mitigated a deadly psychological danger to the individual, now encourages the creation of a society which is dedicated to the prevention of transgression, rather than to its punishment. To maintain the integrity of the society requires the nurturance of its members, rather than their destruction. In short, the Superego is the psychological model of a civilization. We shall discuss the positive or social aspects of the Superego in the chapter on the Sense of Justice.

Social Controls

The development of a system of social controls takes place in two phases. The first phase consists of repression both of Oedipal behavior and of Oedipal fantasy. Repression, we recall, consists of the allocation to unawareness of a feeling, thought, or act, without the subject being consciously aware of the process or its immediate result. Oedipal behavior consists of the child engaging the principal energies of his parent figure of the opposite sex, in a fashion which is similar to a love relationship of adult life, and Oedipal fantasy is the fantasying of this behavior. Relics of this phase in adult life are seen in a woman saying, "But Daddy knows best," or a man, "There's nothing as good as home cooking."

In the second phase, the repression which we saw above in the first phase is replaced by the formation of a "Sense of Justice," which is a moral scheme of controls. This sense of justice originates psychologically as an unconscious striving toward a code of contractual equality, and in its functioning, generates positive social intercourse. It is not dominated by totalitarian figures, as is the psychology of the nursery, but instead grants equal rights to all, regardless of their power. It is not continually under repression, as is the Oedipus Complex, which is permitted a conscious appearance only in disguised forms. Instead, the Sense of Justice achieves relatively direct conscious expression, for we discuss it in the form of principles of fairness, tabulation of rights, and the rules of law.

By means of such codification, the individual's sense of justice may communicate directly with that of others in the community. This communication, which is a form of social intercourse, yields pleasure through its relief of emotional tensions. At the same time, the sharing of a code with others, and their acceptance of the credo, brings with it a pleasurable reaffirmation of the faith. The positive side of the sense of justice is expressed in this communication.

This sense of justice, particularly well described by Alexander (2), is a sociopsychological phenomenon, then, which develops in the latency period — between the beginning of the Oedipus period and the onset of adolescence. Once developed, it persists actively within the individual throughout his life with such strength and pervasiveness that it becomes a part of the culture of which that individual is a member. In the last chapter, we shall describe details of the social and historical development of the Sense of Justice.

The remaining sociopsychological phases of development — adolescence, adulthood and senescence — will also be presented with the aid both of certain physiological observations, and studies of psychological material. We shall note how as the individual maturates he becomes more complex, as does the society in which he moves. It is the interchange between the complexity of the individual and the complications of societal living with which we are most vitally concerned.

ADOLESCENCE

While adolescence may be defined chronologically as the age period which includes the thirteenth through the nineteenth years, or sociologically as a phase of turmoil for the rapidly growing young person, for his stability-seeking family, and for his troubled society, a simple and basic definition can be made in biologic terms. Biologically, adolescence is the era of maximum body growth and of maximum increment of sexual characteristics, including the ability to fertilize, to become fertilized and to bear young.

The differences between the sexual characteristics of the adolescent male and the adolescent female are most striking to the objective observer. As a harbinger of the differences in sexuality between mature men and women, the sex pattern of the adolescent male already shows marked divergences from that of his female contemporary. The average American boy begins adolescence in the eighth grade, according to the studies of Kinsey (51) and his collaborators, who used the criteria of adolescence that were reported most frequently by their subjects: the appearance of pubic hair, first ejaculation, change in voice, increase in rate of body growth, and completion of growth in stature.

Ejaculation, which appeared at an average age of thirteen years and seven months, is not only a notable event in the psychology of the young male, but is also a sociologic phenomenon of major note, for erections followed by ejaculations reach a peak at the age of seventeen, and then gradually diminish, despite the thinly disguised boastfulness of older men in discussions of the "prime of life." (History and folklore give examples to show that there is no substitute for youth, as in a legend of the young Hercules. This truly heroic figure was assigned by King Thesbos, the master of a Mediterranean island, to perform some quite physically taxing duties during the day, and also to impregnate all of his forty-nine daughters by night, all in the span of one week. Hercules completed these chores on schedule. Fifty-one babies were born appropriately thereafter, and the island was named, not inappropriately, Sardinia.)

On the distaff side, the young female, who has begun her menstrual periods at an average age of about twelve years, becomes fertile at thirteen, comparable to the male. But orgastic patterns differ markedly. The male normally requires ejaculation in order to experience the sexual orgasm, after which there is a refractory period that persists for a few minutes, even in the adolescent male. During this refractory period, ejaculation is impossible, and even erection is difficult or impossible to achieve. The female, however, shows a distinctively different picture. The female is capable of repeated orgasm, according to the detailed studies of Masters and Johnson (52), going from one orgasm to the next, without a refractory period, and without even a diminution in the level of excitement (63).

Frequently a rate of six orgasms per hour can be attained in adolescence, and maintained without loss through the subsequent years. With appropriate stimulation, some females show a continued sequencing of orgasms, without interruption, for which the clinical term of *status orgasmus* has been devised, (a term similar to *status epilepticus,* in which there are convulsions without interruption).

When the frequency of appearance of a first orgasm at different ages is compared in the Kinsey studies on males and females, there is again a striking difference. By fifteen years of age, ninety-two percent of the boys had had a first orgasm, but at that same age only one-quarter of the females had followed suit. As they grew older, more women reported having had an orgasm, but it was not until women reached an average age of twenty-nine that the occurrence of this event equalled that for boys of fifteen! These data, which were collected in the monumental work of Kinsey and his coinvestigators about a generation ago, may no longer reflect an accurate picture of such differences between the male and the female teenager. This generation has experienced a marked increase in sexual permissiveness for adolescents; with this there has been such an increase in conscious emphasis on sexuality that many have accused today's society of fostering a race of sexual athletes. With greater sexual freedom, which permits the female to explore and experiment more fully, clinical experience suggests that the adolescent female has now begun to experience orgasm as frequently as her male contemporary.

The social consequences of the adolescents' sexuality are weighty, particularly when we view the adolescents' contribution to the structure of his or her own family. The median age of girls in the United States at the time of marriage is now nineteen years. About one third of the marriages in these teen years are complicated by pregnancy, supplementing the item that most illegitimate births occur in teenagers. About one half of teen marriages end in divorce, this being twice the rate of the population in general.

The psychological concomitants of the teenager's sexuality are equally vexatious. In adolescence, we see the teenage individual actively engaged in testing his controls and of finding the limits of his freedoms, as he develops his strengths. Because of this, adolescence is notable for its rebelliousness to authority, for radical idealism, for quick changes from one extreme to another, for intellectual hunger and experiment, a passion for intense emotional experiences, for its emotional upheavals, for a powerful revival of sexual preoccupations which are associated with adult-like sexual behavior, and for its romantic infatuations.

The psychological diagnosis of the teenager, whether this diagnosis is being made for the court or for any other entity in the community, must take into account these remarkable instabilities of adolescence. The policy and procedure by which the adolescent tests reality and tests fantasy, must be compared not only with the substance and style of the self-acknowledged mature man, but primarily and basically with the approach to reality testing and fantasy testing that is used by his adolescent peers.

Further, the socio-cultural background of the adolescent adds its distinctive coloration to his emotional picture. In the "lower class" groups, as contrasted to those of the middle class, for example, there are marked differences in sexual behavior and feelings, matters which we have seen to express much of the adolescent's energies. The lower class groups show "segregation" of females from males, so that the sexes are separate in many of their activities of daily living and of pleasure-seeking (20, 79, 96). In the middle class a more conjugal relationship between men and women is maintained, which results in a greater sharing by the sexes of time and energy, and in the inculcation of this ethic into the growing individual. Directly related to this class difference is the greater amount of homosexual behavior among adolescent males in the lower class, as contrasted in the middle class adolescent to a lesser amount of homosexual activity, which is coupled with a guilty fear of homosexuality.

Perhaps the variety and intensity of their concerns impelled a calm and wise student of young people, Anna Freud, to write, "Adolescence is by its nature an interruption of peaceful growth, and the upholding of a steady equilibrium during the adolescent process is in itself abnormal" (23).

CHAPTER 3

ADULTHOOD

"The mature, the professional and the wise are aware of self, allow for weakness, and maintain equilibrium" (31).

Unlike the law, which sets exact chronological limits on the onset of adulthood, the disciplines of medicine, psychiatry and psychology cannot be so specific. Instead, scholars in these fields suggest that adulthood is equivalent to maturity, to normalcy or mental health. Yet each one of these terms differs from the other, as will shortly be shown. In addition, the imprecisions of terminology are compounded by the concoction of a philological complex such as "mature adulthood" or "adult normal happiness," as in this (70) instance:

"But the rewards of mature adulthood are worth it all. The mature adult knows a sacred cow when he sees one. He can distinguish between a Principle with a capital P and an absurd myth more accepted than questioned. He knows the difference between what he wants to do and what he is merely supposed to do. He knows that first things come first, and he knows what his own first things are. He knows himself, he knows his world, and more — he knows an ethical, responsible, and joyous way for him to live in it."

This demonstration of freeing oneself from old clichés by means of coining new ones will be taken up in a later chapter, on Normalcy, under the heading of value judgements.

In our search for definition, however, we receive some help from etymology, for the word adult, modified from modern

43

French, is represented in Latin as *adultus,* which in turn is the past participle of *adolescere,* meaning to grow up. Nevertheless, etymological references almost universally cite legal definitions of the word adult. These legal descriptions are historical and geographical in origin. Most of them set forth the age at which a person is relieved of the disability of being a child, in the eyes of the law. By direct inference, the relief of this special disability is synchronous with becoming an adult.

But the law attempts to specify the purpose for which this disability is ablated, so that criminal liability begins at the age of seven, fourteen or eighteen years, depending on the customs which concern economic support, marriage or economic responsibility, while the liability to be bound by a contract generally begins at fourteen. Most often, an individual legally becomes an adult in the span between his twelfth and his twenty-fifth birthdays. Thus, in the Anglo Saxon common law, based in the times when a boy was no longer a minor after he became strong enough to operate a plow, and the life expectancy was less than 30 years, a male became an adult for many purposes at 14 and a female at 12. But in the Mohammedan code, despite its granting of lesser rights for women, both males and females become adults at the same age of 15. Some of the United States consider women to be adult at age 18, while others follow the general pattern by which both sexes are considered to be adults at 21. In still other states, a lack of clarity exists as to whether a young female who is married, should be treated as a juvenile or as an adult. Unfortunately, we do not have a uniform legal code which proclaims the age at which the individual is no longer a child.

But biological science takes a simpler and precise approach. The beginning of adulthood, as seen by biology, is represented by the onset of the capacity to reproduce. If we apply this test to human individuals, we shall ascribe adulthood to 13-year-old boys and girls, an age which was considered adult for some purposes in bygone times, but is not generally applicable today.

A confirmatory criterion which biology uses to establish adulthood is the achievement of full stature. In the human species, the completion of growth in body height takes place at 17 years. This is the median age of consent for sexual purposes in the U.S., the range being from 14 to 21, but it is not sufficient to be considered adult by the populace at large. In these two examples, a biological maturity has been reached in the maturation of the human individual, concomitantly with the attainment of the legal age of adulthood. But when we examine these examples we see that when these biological and legal standards have been passed, the psychological achievements of adulthood which are required by today's society and technology have not yet been acquired.

From biology, we shall turn directly to psychology, for going beyond the sociological approach, the disciplines of psychology and psychiatry orient themselves on the individual's mental state, yet simultaneously deal with the dynamic system of that individual's human and material environment. Psychologists often test the dynamic adaptation of an individual in his environment. Thus, one psychological definition states that adulthood begins with the attainment of a high level of ability to perform psychological adaptation. This is the basis for a definition both of maturity and psychological health, given by the World Federation of Mental Health Commission (100): "To possess sufficient insight into motivations, capacities and shortcomings; and to construct life goals in keeping with internal and external reality."

An equally broad but more biological approach was taken by Hsu (48) who in essence proposed that the biologically mature man strives for

1. Sustenance
2. Sexuality

and also is impelled toward

3. Socializing
4. Security
5. Status

but that in our Western culture, mature individuals also trend toward the

6. Creative urge, or a movement in the direction of new experiences.

A scholarly psychologist, who performed classical and original studies on his subjects, equated maturity with adultness (41) and then offered several definitions of maturity. From an early study, he suggested in a rather attractive psychodynamic definition, that

"Maturity is the predominance of the efficient, the discriminating, the differentiated and the realistic, over the primitive, the impulsive and the passionate."

Later, as a distillate of his extensive testing on college students, he set forth the trends of the mature person.

Heath stated that the mature man or woman
   1. Experiences a successful long term adaptation, even though short term maladaptation may occur.
   2. Shows a mature style of mastering problems.
   3. His state of organization improves with age.
   4. He shows long-term goal directed behavior.
   5. He is reality oriented, socially adaptable, and self-confident.

He then studied in detail the traits which are said by various groups to comprise the essentials of maturity. These essential components are paraphrased here:

THE COMPONENTS OF MATURITY

REALISTIC judgement: judicious; objective; faces reality
SOCIAL feeling: warmth; compassion for others; kindness; friendly
CAPABLE of personal love: deep friendships; tenderness; personal involvement
ADAPTABLE: can postpone own needs to adjust; harmonizes others' needs and own
INTEGRATED: balanced; harmonious; unity; consistency
SELF-RELIANT: self-sufficient; sense of autonomy; independent
SELF-CONTROL: does not get upset easily; tolerates frustration; can control emotion
SELF-ACCEPTANCE: self-respect; self-trust; respects, values others and their opinions — tolerant; considerate of others' rights; accepts others' limitations
STRONG values: meaning or direction to life; stands up for convictions; develops a philosophy of life
INTEGRITY: sincerity; holds to word; honest; acts out of own being
CREATIVE: productive generativity
OPENNESS to new experience: receptive to ideas; new growth
WIDE interests: self extended into many activities
ALTRUISTIC: gives to and serves others and their welfare
SENSITIVE: aware of others and to experience
HAPPY marriage: happy family life; close family; loving parent
EMPATHIC: intuitive; insightful into others' lives; understanding of others

In this controlled study, Heath compared the traits of maturity that had been suggested by psychologists, with the traits that were proposed by three other groups. These groups were the students' professors, the students themselves, and his own research team.

(These classifications cover a wide range of expertise, certainly including that of a lawyer or of any professional person). He found that there was excellent agreement among all groups on the presence or absence of maturity in his subjects. Thus the experts, the professional psychologists and the college students, all agreed on the characteristics of maturity.

Teachers' definitions of maturity are also strikingly similar to their concept of the end product of their primary goal — a man who is well educated. The trustees of the Carnegie Foundation for the Advancement of Teaching (13) have summarized their aim very clearly:

> "Educators will compile different lists of the qualities which charac-
> terize an educated man, but the lists will be neither as long nor as
> conflicting as one might suppose. Most of us agree that we would
> wish the educated man to be marked by intellectual curiosity, the
> capacity to think critically, and the capacity to weigh evidence
> dispassionately. We would wish him to be tolerant, temperate, bal-
> anced in judgment; and we would wish him to possess certain general
> qualities such as maturity, magnanimity, and so forth. We would not
> wish him to be intellectually lazy or slovenly, and we would not
> wish his rational processes to be at the mercy of his fears and
> prejudices."

This raises a basic question — can an individual learn to be mature? My answer is "yes." We can learn to listen and to see more fully and more clearly, and we can learn how better to perceive our motivations and the motivations of others.

> And we can learn in a great many areas of performance, to
> function more forcefully, more efficiently and more satisfyingly.
> Even in psychiatric therapy, which is called upon primarily not to
> study normal reaction patterns, but instead for treatment of subjec-
> tive or objective disorders of adaptation, the process of learning
> plays a significant role. In most forms of psychotherapy, the success-
> ful patient learns from a self-improvement program. Even in psycho-
> analysis, which was designed to perceive and conquer the barriers to
> progress which are in the unconscious, Freud described the useful-
> ness of teaching the analysand a certain amount of psychological
> dynamics.*

The contribution of psychoanalysis to the concept of adultness should be of additional value, for two of the most significant

*Freud wrote (28): "Thus psychoanalytic treatment acts as a second education of the adult, as a correction to his education as a child."

themes in psychoanalysis are its practical clinical organization, and its penetration into the unconscious. It was the clinician's sense of practicality which prompted Freud, when asked for the characteristics of a mature man, to say, "To be able to love, and to be able to work." Yet these two abilities, which are consciously noted so often, have major meanings in the unconscious of the normal man.

The ability to work requires the development of an Ego that is oriented toward external reality, yet is able to integrate the impulses that arise both from the Id and from the Superego, in a functional fashion. Working in a civilized society requires working with others, which in turn calls for identification with peers, superiors and subordinates, as well as the transformation of inacceptable thought or behavior into productivity. And perhaps most significantly, the performance of productive work in the community demonstrates the result of two pieces of psychological work: The reawakening of an identification with an authority figure (or a father image), and simultaneously the ability through work, to give a gift of love.

By being "able to love", Freud referred to his observations on psychologically mature love. In these histories, he showed that the early phases of psychosexual maturation, going through the oral (or intestinal) phase, the anal, the phallic and the latency phases, had successively been displaced from primacy by the genital, or mature phase. Each one of these earlier phases symbolizes a set of physiological and psychological functions in the striving for pleasure, and each one is competent at the age in which it is dominant, to produce pleasure at the pre-adult level. In addition, these early stages leave their functioning traces in the adult personality, in much the way as the anatomy and chemistry of the adult contains traces of the ingredients of his origin from lower forms of life. Yet these earlier phases not only radiate about a non-genital zone of the body, but also focus on an organ system of the individual's own body.

The genital phase of psychosexual maturation, as will be seen from a review of the section on the Oedipal period, is different from its predecessors in both of these respects: In the genital phase, the organ which achieves primacy as the symbol of psychologic expression is the organ which achieves its biological maturity later than all of its precursors. Secondly, in the genital phase, the direction of the individual's drive for pleasure is reversed from being directed inward, toward himself, to being directed outward, toward another person. This genital functioning, particularly within the phenomenon of love, thus symbolizes the complex behaviors of interpersonal intercourse.

But phallic activity, as exemplified by masturbation, differs in these two respects from genital activity, as represented by tender intercourse. In the adult female, the phallus which is stimulated is the body of the clitoris, which permits her to experience many repeated orgasms (63) without the collaboration of any other person, except in fantasy. Psychologically mature genital activity, as we above define it in the adult female, however, can result in stimulation of the vagina, thereby secondarily stimulating the clitoris, but also requires the functioning of the genital of the male. His functioning adds the impact of his personality to her fantasy.

In addition, every act of tender intercourse results in the mutual participation in fantasy by the two partners. In the course of this participation, both the man and the woman become players in the basic drama of man — the Oedipal romance — in which pursuit is followed by possession, to be succeeded by the sharing of a regression to pure pleasure.

Following Freud's researches, many maps of adulthood have been drawn. The most practical of these are the clinical outlines which give those positive features of adult life that we wish to augment, along with the negative features that we wish to diminish. One of the best of these outlines is that of Abrahamsen (1965) (1).

SPECIFIC YARDSTICK
FOR SELF-EXPLORATION

Since your emotional comfort rests on your degree of emotional maturity, I have set down here, as a specific guide in your self-exploration, a more detailed list of (a) feelings and actions that express emotional maturity, and (b) stumbling blocks to emotional maturity which we reproduce here, showing the adult with his psychologically mature features on one side, while on the other side of the ledger, are the difficulties which derive from expressions of earlier phases than the adult, or the immature.

(Specific Yardstick for
Self-Exploration by David
Abrahamsen, M.D.)

**Feelings and Actions That Express
Emotional Maturity**

A. *Ability to Give and Accept Love and Affection*

1. Feeling free to please yourself as well as others — ability to pay compliments or extend gifts or favors without desire for personal gain
2. Realistic appreciation of yourself: expanding or limiting your own activities according to each situation — being a leader or follower without feeling emotionally uncomfortable
3. Freedom to accept enjoyment and pleasure and feeling entitled to it for a job well done
4. Ability to accept compliments and praise without feeling uncomfortable or letting it go to your head
5. Ability to take orders without feeling "pushed around" — ability to express yourself in words as well as in action, without feeling guilty — ability to give orders without fear of being disliked — ability to risk the chance of failure — ability to cope with failure and rebound
6. Knowledge that love is important but not the all-encompassing solution to everything
7. Feeling confident enough to create your own chances and to accept opportunities when they present themselves

B. *Independence and Adult Behavior*

1. Selflessness
   a. Ability to share your loved ones and your material possessions without feeling threatened — genuine desire to give as well as take — regard for the needs of others, with ability to forego gratification of your own satisfactions, when necessary
   b. Realistic appraisal of yourself, your life situation, your capabilities — belief in yourself
   c. Realistic evaluation of your family's short-comings, while

(Continued on page 52)

Reprinted with permission from *The Road to Emotional Maturity,* by David Abrahamsen, M.D., published by Prentice-Hall, New York, 1965.

Stumbling Blocks to Reaching
Emotional Maturity

(Related largely to fixations in the Oral Stage)

A. *Excessive Need for Love and Affection*

1. Need to please others: "buying" friendship — flattering others (hoping to win their favor)
2. Under-estimation of yourself: assuming role of not being important — limiting your own activities — playing "second fiddle" — taking a "back seat" — becoming subservient to others (often leads to feeling resentful or hostile, feeling of being "used")
3. Excessive tendency toward doing things for others or working harder, as a means of compensating for unworthiness (leading to masochism or "Martyr" Complex)
4. Tearing yourself down (so that others won't have a chance to do so, or in hopes that they will praise you instead) — inability to accept praise
5. Fear of authority — fear of success or failure — fear of asserting yourself (because you may be rejected or punished)
6. Belief that "love solves all problems"
7. Feeling sorry for yourself — feeling that you "have no luck"

B. *Dependency and Childishness*

1. Egocentricity
   a. Possessiveness — feeling "everything is mine" — jealousy — not wanting to give or to share loved ones or personal belongings
   b. Lack of realism about yourself and your life situation — over or under evaluation of your capabilities
   c. Exalted opinion of your own family, through need for prestige — under-estimation of your family

(Continued on page 53)

       still accepting them — feeling of being recognized in your own right

  d. Knowledge of your capabilities without need of convincing others — ability to appraise correctly your own accomplishments — appreciation of sincere praise — ability to be in the limelight without being fearful or becoming overly self-impressed

  e. Ability to work at full capacity, based on realistic appraisal of your own mental and emotional capabilities, without driving yourself to out-do others

  f. Realistic self-esteem

  g. Even disposition, calmness, with ability to express anger when necessary and to fight for your rights — ability to follow your own wishes and desires without using this to hurt someone — recognition that revenge is a negative form of satisfaction — accepting responsibility for your own mistakes

2. Freedom from need to dominate others — without loss of ability for leadership when needed

  a. Ability to recognize and accept situations beyond your control — recognition of your own limitations

  b. Ability to withstand and to admit defeat, without permitting it to dampen your spirit

  c. Willingness to admit "moral weaknesses" and willingness to change

  d. Regard for individuality of others — lack of need to out-smart others (through not feeling controlled by them)

  e. Modesty in attitude and actions — feeling emotionally comfortable even when the attention is directed toward others

  f. Allowing others to be themselves

3. Responsibility — wanting to grow up

  a. Self-reliance — making genuine efforts before seeking help — asking for help directly

  b. Feeling genuinely independent — welcoming responsibility and accepting help with it when offered or necessary

4. Active participation in life

  a. Awareness of things around you and ability to enjoy them — genuine enthusiasm and spontaneity, as opposed to boredom

(Continued on page 54)

  d. Self-praise — bragging — falling for flattery — namedropping
  e. Excessive ambitions
  f. Excessive pride
  g. Excessive hostility and hate — rebelliousness and revengefulness — irritability — tendency to blame others

2. Need to control others — through fear of being controlled
  a. Feeling of omnipotence — lack of humility
  b. Having to win, to be "the best"
  c. Self-righteousness — need to be morally right
  d. Contempt for others — calculating, cunning behavior
  e. Seeking attention (monopolizing conversations, situations, and so forth)
  f. Nagging

3. Wanting to be taken care of — without genuine desire to reciprocate
  a. Acting helpless, babyish — feeling "Mother will always help me" or that "no one ever helps me" — whining or complaining
  b. Taking on tasks to prove your independence, while resenting and feeling hostile about it, often refusing help when offered
4. Undue passivity
  a. Letting life pass you by without participating actively — need to prove your aggressiveness to cover up this passivity (the struggle between passivity and activity leading to indecisiveness)

(Continued on page 55)

    b. Realization of your own ability to take care of yourself
       and others — being resourceful, able to meet situations
       adequately or to seek advice or help if necessary

5. Feeling of being accepted, of belonging
    a. Ability to realize and accept the fact that not everyone
       will like you — ability to spend time alone without feel-
       ing uneasy — feeling at home anywhere, of "belong-
       ing" — feeling accepted for yourself
    b. Feeling of self-confidence — ability to cope with danger
       realistically, in spite of anxiety or fear — realistic trust of
       others

6. Realistic appreciation of your individuality
    a. Ability to make independent decisions with certainty and
       without undue delay — healthy self-assertion
    b. Accepting differences in yourself and others as being
       normal

7. Adult feelings
    a. Realistic awareness of your emotional and physical
       health and requirements
    b. Ability to "wait your turn" — calmness and patience —
       ability to see another point of view — flexibility
    c. Balance of work interspersed with recreation — accepting
       and welcoming responsibility toward yourself and others
       as a challenge to your resourcefulness and a means for
       inner growth — enjoying the present and planning for the
       future
    d. Ability to develop and enjoy new interests — enjoyment
       of life around you
    e. Search for ethical and spiritual values with a real under-
       standing of your place in the universe — seeking deeper
       understanding of yourself and life around you
       8. Ability to work in harmony with others, for mutual
    benefit — ability to do a job well for personal gratification
    rather than for external recognition

9. Constructiveness
    a. Moderation in saving and spending — living within your
       income, while always striving for something better,
       though with a realistic appraisal of your limitations
    b. Enjoyment of material things, with ability to relinquish
       them if necessary

(Continued on page 56)

b. Fear of being deserted and helpless — feeling defenseless — failure to meet situations — lack of resourcefulness — quick acceptance of defeat

5. Feeling of being rejected or neglected — without root in reality

   a. Feeling easily offended — needing to be liked by everyone — fear of or inability to be left alone, because it creates feeling of being unloved — homesickness — feeling of not "belonging," or of not being accepted or liked

   b. Excessive anxiety, worry, fearfulness — suspiciousness, distrust of other people's motives toward you — fear of pain, illness, or death

6. Conformity — following other people's opinions

   a. Suggestibility — self-evaluation or decisions based on other people's, rather than your own judgment — submissiveness

   b. Fear of being different — strong though often unconscious tendency to be different, in order to cover up feelings of dependency and conformity

7. Infantile preoccupations

   a. Over-concern with food, sleep, amusements

   b. Inability to tolerate frustrations — impulsiveness — always wanting your own way

   c. Excessive desire to play rather than to work (being glad when you think "you're getting away with something") — "living for the moment" — irresponsibility

   d. Unduly seeking pleasure and new thrills

   e. Indifference to or dread of spiritual (higher) values — hanging onto religion without true understanding of its meaning and purpose

8. Lack of cooperation with others in groups or work — extreme need for and expectation of recognition and reward for even most minor efforts

(Related largely to fixations in the Anal Stage)

9. Destroying or collecting, controlling

   a. Hoarding (miserliness), or being a spend-thrift (only for yourself)

   b. Excessive desire for possession of material things

(Continued on page 57)

    c. Ability to show love and warmth toward others

    d. Ability to accept criticism without feeling crushed by it but, rather, learning from it — flexibility — ability to grow and change

    e. Willingness to accept the fact that nothing is perfect — feeling free to make the necessary mistakes in the process of learning

10. Acceptance of parents as a married couple and as parents

    a. Realistic love and devotion for both parents — ability to form healthy and satisfying relationships with members of both sexes

    b. Appreciation and acceptance of your own value as a member of your sex, and appreciation of value of others — normal sex life

11. Ability to establish close emotional ties with others and still remain independent

    a. Occasional masturbation if unable to find a mate — fondling, kissing, and petting as precursor to sexual intercourse

    b. Occasional "having fun" in terms of sex (dirty jokes, looking at pornographic literature, attending stag parties) but otherwise normal sex life

    c. Love of parents and family without their taking priority in your development of other relationships

   c. Excessive teasing and "practical jokes" — cruelty toward people and animals — sadism

   d. Compulsiveness — rigidity — impatience — ambivalence

   e. Perfectionism (to cover up feeling of inner imperfections) — fear of admitting mistakes, need to be right

(Related largely to fixations in the Oedipal or Electra Stage)

10. Desire to replace parent of same sex

   a. Excessive attachment to parent or members of opposite sex (often resulting in hostility through feeling rejected) — hostility toward, or fear of, parent or members of same sex (often covered up by excessive displays of affection — fear of castration

   b. Competitiveness with parent or members of same sex — inability to decide or accept your role as a male or female — wanting to be a member of the opposite sex — homosexuality, voyeurism, exhibitionism

(Related largely to fixations in the Genital Stage)

11. Fear of emotional involvement — not wanting to be tied down

   a. Excessive masturbation — fondling, kissing, and petting, in preference to sexual intercourse

   b. Voyeurism, exhibitionism, bi-sexuality, homosexuality

   c. Excessive attachment to parents or individual family members or close friends

Thus we have sketched, in outline form, the characteristics of adulthood, as a series of points in life's continuum. The next section will define senescence, and will emphasize some of its positive and negative values.

CHAPTER 4

SENESCENCE
AND THE BRAIN SYNDROME

SENESCENCE

Senescence, or the period during which an individual grows old (14), has attracted the attention of a number of poets, principally in their senior years. Thus, Longfellow wrote

> It is too late! Ah, nothing is too late
> Till the tired heart shall cease to palpitate.
> Cato learned Greek at eighty; Sophocles
> Wrote his grand Oedipus, and Simonides
> Bore off the prize of verse from his compeers,
> When each had numbered more than four-score years,—
>
> Chaucer, at Woodstock with the nightingales,
> At sixty wrote the Canterbury Tales;
> Goethe at Weimar, toiling to the last,
> Completed Faust when eighty years were past.
> These are indeed exceptions; but they show
> How far the gulf-stream of our youth may flow
> Into the arctic regions of our lives.
> For age is opportunity no less
> Than youth itself, tho' in another dress
> And as the evening twilight fades away
> The sky is filled with stars invisible by day.

And then Robert Browning, with less documentation but with more bravura:

Grow old along with me!
The best is yet to be,
The last of life, for which the first was made:
Our times are in His hand
Who saith, "A whole I planned,
Youth shows but half; trust God: see all, nor be afraid!"

While Shakespeare, who at the age of 33 wrote and acted the role of Melancholy Jacques in *As You Like It,* took a less than enthusiastic view of man's aging years. In the speech by Jacques on the seven ages of man, Shakespeare first introduces the age of maturity, which wears judicial robes:

And then the justice,
In fair round belly with good capon lin'd
With eyes severe and beard of formal cut,
Full of wise saws and modern instances;
And so he plays his part.

He then describes the old dotard, or pantaloon, as the senescent age.

The sixt age shifts
Into the lean and slipper'd pantaloon
With spectacles on nose and pouch on side;
His youthful hose well sav'd, a world too wide
For his shrunk shank, and his big manly voice,
Turning again toward childish treble, pipes
And whistles in his sound.

But medical specialists have offered a more modern definition. Senescence is a progressive, irreversible loss of the individual's physical and mental functioning because of his aging, and generally beginning at about age 65, but frequently much earlier or later. Aging, or as our British friends write it, ageing, is a process which continues throughout life, as in the aging of a patina, but is often used synonomously with senescence. We do not yet know the cause of aging, but there are three leading theories to explain this phenomenon in man and animals. In the first, autoimmunization, or the gradual development of an adverse sensitivity to one's own body chemicals; the second states that aging results from a life-long series of minor or major attacks by physical trauma or disease; and the third suggests that the process of aging is in itself a disease.

The scope of the question of senescence is a wide one, for every day in the United States over 1000 individuals reach the age of 65, and can each expect to live an average of about 14 years longer. The expectancy for senior females is considerably higher than for males, so that in the entire group which is older than 65, there are 77 males to every 100 females.

Positive and Negative Features of Senescence

Senescence in otherwise normal individuals has both positive and negative effects on human psychological functioning, of which some intellectual and sexual examples will be given here.

In older people, reaction time — the time between presentation of a stimulus and the moment of the subject's reaction — decreases slowly until about age 50, then slows much more rapidly as the subject ages further. Thus, for physically normal individuals who drive motor vehicles, the time which is required for a driver to react to a stoplight signal has been measured. At the age of 65 this reaction time is about 15% slower than at age 25, and at the speed of closure of two rapidly moving vehicles, this is highly significant. The moment of time which is required to make a simple identification is also longer in older individuals. Thus in a laboratory experiment, a combination of 1, 2, 3 or 4 lamps was illuminated, and the subject was required to report the combination which was displayed. Persons over 65 showed no lack of accuracy, but were slower than the younger subjects. In another older group, perceptions of single items were slower, and learning time was slower.

In association with medical progress, the lives of women have progressively been lengthened, unlike their male counterparts, so that a female child who is born today in the United States is expected to live 74 years. A male child of today has an expectancy of 66.7 years. In keeping with this striking disparity in age of death, men in their advancing years show a fall in their intellectual test functioning below that of women of their same age. This suggests the possibility that in the latter years of life, at least, a match of intellectual functioning can be promoted by a man marrying a woman who is older than he is, rather than younger.

Preservation of Sexual Ability

Between aging men and women, there are marked differences in the maintenance of sexual competence. While a number of men as they age, show partial or total loss of erectal potency, making customary coitus impossible, the older female continues to possess the ability of her younger years to become sexually aroused, to perform sexual intercourse, and to experience orgasm (52, 9, 63). This preservation of sexuality in the aging female, consisting of her capability being undiminished except for reproduction, poses a problem in our culture. We are not at ease with the conscious acceptance of senescent sexuality, and frequently escape into the fiction that older people enter a second age of sexual innocence. By the working of a thinly disguised variety of illogic, we expect that a woman who in her earlier years has developed a fullness and width in range of sexual enjoyment and response, somehow will give up the feelings and behavior of a lifetime of sexual experience when she grows older. It is an expectation that extends throughout the community, so that both the younger and the older individuals feel the conflict between their fantasy wishes and the prohibition by society. Younger persons are critical and verbally derogatory of sexual behavior by older women, while the older women react with frustration, psychic or somatic symptoms and guilt.

But while the older female encounters social and psychological barriers to her expression of sexuality, the senescent male finds that he must contend not only with these barriers, but must also deliver the masculine essential to coitus—a functioning penile erection. In our culture, some disturbance of erection appears in all men at some time, however briefly, in direct relationship to psychological pressures. In addition, the trend of performance over the years, in sexual behaviors that can be quantified, suggests a physical reason for a gradual decline in function with aging, such as the decrease in rapidity of erection or the number of ejaculations. With both psychologic and physiologic factors that can interfere with the erection of the older male, a disorder of erection is quite common. In Kinsey's study (51), 25% of the men who were 65 years of age admitted to having a chronic and total lack of ability to achieve a sexually functioning erection. It is reasonable to expect that at least an additional 25% of men at this age and older actually experience sufficient disturbance of their ability at erection to cause significant discomfort to themselves or to their partners.

Treatment to relieve this distress has varied over the years. In Scripture we see where the aging King David was given a comely young maiden to cheer him and be with him, representing perhaps a early version of modern behavioral therapy (I Kings 1:2). Modern psychiatric theories are utilized to treat the impotent personality, often with improvement of sexual potency. And now a group of researchers who studied the human sexual response in a most highly mechanized laboratory (Masters) report a notable improvement in overall sexual functioning as an offshoot of their physiological studies.

But here we are not primarily concerned with the treatment of sexuality in the senescent individual, for we are concerned primarily with the prevention of such problems. In prevention we may start by eliminating the evil coloration which our society imputes to the sexual wishes of our elders. We may well eliminate the combination of bias with inaccuracy which was occasionally demonstrated by Kinsey (51, p. 237).

"In many older persons, erectile impotence is, fortunately, accompanied by a decline in, and usually complete cessation of erotic response."

And one is equally surprised to see this wise observer (86) both pass moral judgement and also fail to use a legal term correctly.

> "Old men often marry young women. Less frequently, young men marry old women. The law tends to be liberal in such matters and in my experience it is very difficult to get a marriage annulled, once it has been consummated. When an old man marries a young girl, it does not represent the type of affection which is usually designated as married love. The old man wishes either a toy or a pet, or, perhaps a housekeeper. What does the young woman want? Perhaps a father or an older brother, but more often a bank account. This leads to all sorts of unhappiness. It is astonishing how easy it is for utterly incompetent people to get married. It is likewise astonishing how difficult it is to get them separated by law."

Depression in the Aging

Another phenomenon which is significant in older people is the reaction to a personal loss with more severe grief or depression than is seen in younger groups. By loss, we mean the loss of a loved person, or of an abstraction which has taken the place of a loved person, such as one's country, the abstraction of liberty, or an ideal (26). Grief is primarily a normal reaction of sadness, precipitated by the loss of an object and focussed principally on that object. Grief does not produce disorganization of the personality, and in many cases, improves without specialized interference in 4-6 weeks. Mourning is a close relative of grief.

Depression, however, is a pathologically sad state in which the object which is lost is not clearly or consciously seen. There are multiple physical manifestations, such as general weakness, hypertension, awakening at 4 A.M. and other misleading physical symptoms which may result mistakenly in a primary somatic diagnosis. In depression, the personality suffers disorganization to a certain extent, with the appearance, particularly in older women, of paranoid delusions. In addition, the ego becomes paralyzed, and in extreme cases the wish to live is replaced by the wish to die.

Suicide is thus a possibility in depression, appearing most frequently in senescence and senectitude. The following table shows the sixfold increase in suicide with age.

Age	Rate of Suicide per 1000 individuals
20	6.4
60 – 69	30.0
85 +	39.0

Age also increases the proportion of males who commit suicide.

Age	Ratio of male suicides to female
Below 70 years	3.5 / 1
Above 70 years	10 / 1

With these items from the clinician's notebook, which were given here because they are clinical guideposts for counselors, and therefore useful to counselors at law, we shall go on to the positive aspects of senescence.

Positive Aspects

1. Education Produces an Increase in IQ

Over many years, tests which obtain an IQ from the general public had shown that:
   a. The intelligence rises rapidly to the age of 16 years
   b. The rate of increase in intelligence diminishes during years 18-21
   c. After age 21, the total intelligence, not the rate of increase, begins a slow and gradual decline, so that for many of us at age 55 the intelligence has fallen to the 14 year level.
   d. In the advanced years, after senescence has merged into senility or senectitude, a rapid decline in intellectual function takes place.

But in a group of men who were wounded in World War II and had received training, remediation or further education, a fifteen-year study showed that all (except those wounded in the prime language center of the brain) demonstrated an increase in intelligence. In another follow-up study in which men were tested twenty years after the original test, those who had completed a greater number of years of schooling made higher scores on the second test than did the men who had previously been their intellectual equals, but who had completed less schooling. In a group of 127 men who had taken an intelligence test in the course of an entrance examination for Iowa State College, these men were given the same test, thirty years later. There was a significant increase in their total scores, in which particular gains were made in the subtests of Practical Judgement, Information and Analogies. (Lorge). In addition, "the more formal education each individual had, the greater the probability of a gain on the retest."

Thus in the testing which is described above, all of which having been done with the Army Alpha, which is a practical type of intelligence test, the *intelligence increases with education.*

Education Prevents Senescence

Since continued education in the adult is associated not only with protection against the expected amount of decline in intelligence over the years, but accompanies an actual gain in IQ, we are prompted to ask a related question. Does not education also afford protection against the intellectual deficits of senescence? In a summary of a thorough review of the literature, Busse (12) reported that education not only is a safeguard against the expected intellectual deficits that develop in senescence, but also assists the aging individual to adapt successfully to his own environment, being notably successful in avoiding the necessity of hospitalization.

A higher educational level in the senescent citizen is associated with a higher level of general performance in his environment. The more educated older person is more likely to be able to live in his own home, or his childrens' homes, while his less educated age peer is more likely to need institutional care. This finding is closely related to the observation that older individuals of lower social and economic status (in which education plays a part) show an earlier and faster decline in intellectual functioning, more so for men than for women. In addition, the aging individual who has had a poorer job and a poorer income is more nearly prone to develop the physical disorders and disabilities of age.

Here we have a strong indication of the value of more education during their younger years, for individuals who are now approaching old age. Thus a more extensive formal education during our youth, with the successful inculcation of the desire to learn, will protect us against both mental and physical disorders in our age. This is a potential for the greater strength of our community, which deserves, I feel, a very high priority for vigorous development.

Now we shall describe an abnormal condition in senescence, which increases in incidence with the aging years, so that it occurs in every case of senility—the Brain Syndrome.

THE BRAIN SYNDROME

The brain syndrome is an integrated aggregation of objective signs and symptoms, due to a disturbance in the function of the brain, which produces a diagnostically distinctive diminution in intellectual abilities, as well as a nonspecific disturbance of affect and of behavior. The brain syndrome is thus a psychological disorder that is due to a cerebral disorder. But the psychological pattern is unique, enabling us to distinguish the phenomena of the brain syndrome from those which are seen in those psychological disorders, such as hysteria, the neuroses and most of the psychoses in which no disorder of the brain has been described.

Its scope is great, both in hospitals and in the community. Four-fifths of all first admissions of persons over 65 to public mental hospitals in the United States show the brain syndrome. The resident population in such hospitals of individuals of all ages with a brain syndrome is about 1 million. It is estimated that there is an equal number of subjects with this disorder in nursing homes and similar institutions. In addition, it is likely that in the community at large there are about as many persons with a brain syndrome as those who are institutionalized but who make an adequate adaptation most of the time, or are unable or unwilling to accept institutionalization.

History and Terminology

The history of detailed interest in the brain syndrome is a relatively recent one. Bleuler in 1924 described the psychological manifestations of the brain disease and brain trauma under the heading of the "organic syndrome." Bleuler emphasized that in brain pathology, prominent signs included defects of memory for recent events, defects of retention, of apperception (or the active perception of the environment conjointly with perception of oneself) and of orientation in the environment.

Memory has been divided into four phases:
1. Registration, which is primarily perception of a stimulus.
2. Retention, which is the ability to report a stimulus accurately, immediately after the stimulus is terminated. Example: "Repeat the following digits after I read them to you, but repeat them backwards: 42573." (Rate—one digit per second, no grouping, drop voice only on last digit.)
3. Recall, which is the ability to report a stimulus at a time later than immediately following termination of the stimulus, when

that stimulus is only generally described to the examinee. *Example:* "Now from memory only, draw the designs which you copied from my cards a few minutes ago."

4. Recollection, which is the restitution to memory that takes place on the re-presentation of the original stimulus, resulting in the subject achieving memory of the original stimulus in its original setting.

In 1942, Goldstein (34), who had followed a series of patients with irreversible brain injuries during the war, added many astute clinical observations to our knowledge of brain disorders, and also contributed two terminological tools with which to describe them. Goldstein noted that the abstract attitude, which he called the categorical attitude, was defective in the brain injured patient, in that such a patient had lost some of his capacity to make abstractions. Secondly, Goldstein noted the proneness of brain damaged individuals to react to excessive stress by exhibiting what he called the catastrophic reaction. The catastrophic reaction is a somatic and psychic reaction which is in excess in intensity to that which is required for the stimulus, and is maladaptive as well, for it is at a lower level of adaptive development than is required. Thus an individual who had a defect in recent memory due to brain disease could not find his keys, then upbraided persons who were near him for stealing the keys, and then fell into a crying rage.

In 1944 Reusch (98), who used a group of easily administered psychological tests to follow a series of patients with relatively mild head injuries from the phase of injury through the stage of recovery, emphasized an additional parameter in diagnosis.

Ruesch had pointed out (98) that the psychological signs and symptoms parallel the neurological and other physical indices, in cases which progress from a mild brain syndrome, to confusion through stupor to coma and death. He also emphasized this parallelism of mental and brain signs in persons who recover, an event which took place in a large proportion of his patients' changes in status.

Recovery, or at least improvement in the brain syndrome, is a regular and expected feature of the disorder. In a standard diagnostic manual, (4) this is emphasized by the separation of the "organic brain syndrome" into two principal forms—the chronic, in which restitution does not take place, and the acute, in which recovery is the rule.

Short term changes also regularly take place. Just as most of us become "absent minded" for psychological reasons, at least on a few occasions, the same variety of short term psychological pressures causes the person with a brain syndrome to function less well. But in the brain syndrome, adverse psychic forces may be associated with a worsening to such an extent that disorientation and delirium may result.

In health, there are fluctuations in performance and feeling which follow a regular or irregular pattern, while in disease, particularly in disease of the nervous system, this pattern is exaggerated, both in duration and extent. Thus an individual who had suffered a mild cerebral thrombosis, producing a stroke, fluctuated in function, showing a positive Babinski sign (or positive Babinski test) at one time, and the negative at others, while he also showed marked fluctuations in affect and memory.

Other terms which describe the brain syndrome have appeared in the literature of the health professions, education and the law. What is now defined as the organic brain syndrome (in which the organ concerned is the brain) had been noted as "organic mental syndrome" by the American Psychiatric Association during the year 1933-1952. From 1952-1967, the expression "Brain Disorders" was used, these being divided into acute and chronic brain disorders. The adjectives acute and chronic, which usually signify shortness or length of duration, were defined differently. An acute brain disorder was one "from which the patient recovers" and the chronic brain disorder results from a relatively permanent, more or less irreversible, diffuse impairment of cerebral tissue function." In 1968, a scholarly committee of the American Psychiatric Association supplied a new diagnostic manual, replacing the description "Brain Disorders" with "Organic Brain Syndrome," as above noted, but continuing to qualify acute and chronic not in terms of the passage of time, but of recovery.

Older terms that are noteworthy include organic dementia ("dementia" is literally a loss of mind) to depict a deterioration of intellectual function due to brain disease that is both severe and irreversible. Organic dementia must clearly be separated from dementia praecox—literally, an insanity of juveniles—a term originated by Krepelin in 1896, but replaced in 1920 by Bleuler's term Schizophrenia.

The terms "brain damaged" or "minimal brain damage" have become associated with a syndrome known as Learning Disability or Language Impairment. In such cases of learning disorders, the damage to the brain is so slight as to be detectable only by specialized clinical testing, and many individuals respond satisfactorily to preventive or remedial training. The last term that we shall note here is "pseudo-dementia" or the balderdash syndrome. This is also known as the Ganser syndrome, after Sigbert Josef Maria Ganser, a psychiatrist in Dresden in 1892. Ganser had studied prisoners, malingerers and psychopaths. The appellation of balderdash was attached by English-speaking students of the subject when it was learned that a classical question was answered by the person who evidenced this syndrome, in a characteristic fashion.

Q. How many legs does a three-legged stool have?
A. Four!

In the Ganser syndrome the patient frequently simulates mental retardation, or psychological or neurological disorders of other varieties, in relation to escaping imprisonment. (61) Thus in a citizen who originally was mildly mentally retarded, and also was psychopathic and recently suffered a head injury in association with allegedly committing a criminal act, the addition of a bit of the balderdash syndrome poses a stimulating challenge to the specialist in forensic psychiatry.

Etiology of the Brain Syndrome

The cause of an individual Brain Syndrome is best classified by following the basic classifications of disease that are used in medicine—is it due to physical trauma, intoxication with chemicals, blood vessel disease, psychogenic causes, etc? In a search for causal classification, it is worthy of note that in the brain syndrome, we typically find multiple etiologies in any one person.

Thus an older person with cardiac and cerebral blood vessel disease that is sufficiently severe to produce a brain syndrome may injure his head. Examination may then show a brain syndrome.

The diagnosis gives the predisposing cause as vascular disease, and the precipitating cause as injury.

Diagnosis of the Brain Syndrome

A. Intellectual Functions
   1. Preserved Intellectual Functions

In the brain syndrome characteristically, the store of general information and the vocabulary are well preserved until a severe syndrome has developed. Thus a 67-year-old engineer with mild coronary artery disease had retired two years previously, then had increasing difficulty with memory, such as forgetting where he had put his shopping list, then his spectacles, etc. Yet he was able to give a quite full description of the geography of the U.S.– Mexican border, in which he had been professionally interested, and to use a full lexicon correctly.

Another feature of the mentation which remains intact until quite late is orientation as it is tested in the course of an ordinary clinical examination. In such an examination, the orientation to time, to place and to person is generally scrutinized by inquiring the date or time of day, the name of the structure in which the patient is located, and his name.

Concerning orientation to time, many individuals who show no signs of a brain syndrome are frequently unsure of the date, or beset by recurrent inaccuracy, and may have only a general idea of the time of day. On orientation to place, many persons who are free of a brain syndrome, especially those with less than 6 grades of education and an IQ below 70 (98) do not formulate an objectively standardizable description of locations. Many such persons in a state of health will locate a structure by its subjective use to them, occasionally adding gratuitously that "you can't miss it." Orientation to person is usually tested by asking the patient to give his name, and also to name the examiner, who in the practice of the amenities and for clinical reasons has introduced himself before beginning the history and examination. But in thirty years of practice I have been able to find only one patient who was principally suffering from a brain syndrome who was unable to give his own name recognizably (this was a 60-year arteriosclerotic alcoholic woman who perseverated her own first name, without stammer or tremor in the vocal organs, at the same rate as her Parkinsonian tremor of the extremities). As for remembering the new doctor's name, this is not easy for many of us, when reinforcement of memory is not utilized. In addition, psychic tensions diminish the efficiency of remembering names, as many have noted after seeing embarrassing pauses that take place during social introductions by normally functioning people.

These tensions in the brain syndrome patient not only affect the patient, who may have anxiety in relation to his loss of abilities, and to the possibility of commitment, but also the doctor. One such doctor, so skilled and sophisticated as to be able to perceive most accurately, wrote of his tension, "Aged patients can remind us of our parents, and very likely of our inevitable mortality, especially if we have lost a parent figure. They deny our importance, rip holes in our omniscience and show little promise of being grateful. They do not excite or arouse us, but they constantly threaten to dirty our skins or our clothing and to blemish our record of medical success" (101).

2. Defective Intellectual Functions

On the other hand, those mental functions which are affected earliest in the development of a brain syndrome, and later become the most defective, are the functions of retention and of abstraction. The simplest clinical tests which demonstrate these defects are, in the order of the greatest sensitivity to the least:

1. Subtraction of serial sevens
2. Picture absurdities
3. Visual retention
4. Digit span backwards
5. Picture abstractions

Of these five simple tests, three require the ability to retain information, these three being the serial sevens, visual retention and digit span backwards; while the other two require the exercise of a low order of abstraction—these two being picture absurdities and picture abstractions. However, two of these tests require no special equipment and are valuable in making the diagnosis of a brain syndrome; hence their popularity—the subtraction of serial sevens and the digit span backwards.

a Serial Sevens

The serial sevens should be done in a standarized manner

with a simplified presentation. I use the following. "Take away 7 from 101 (or 99, or 102, etc.) then take away 7 from that number, and continue to take away sevens, giving me the answer each time." Especially for patients who have been tested before, or may be sophisticated in testing or have overlearned the answers, it is advisable not to start with 100, even though this calls for some exercise of mental agility by the examiner.

Since this test requires a spoken presentation and a spoken response, the patient is not to have pencil and paper. However, patients with brain syndromes may count silently with their fingers, often visibly, if one observes for this. Those patients with a brain syndrome and a basal IQ below 75 frequently count downward by ones instead of by sevens, each numerical digit corresponding to a manual digit. But brain syndrome patients with a basal IQ of 110 and above will frequently take away seven mentally without the use of fingers by means of subtracting 5 mentally, and then additionally subtracting 2.

The examiner reads the digits at a rate of one per second, dropping his voice only on the last digit, saying, "I am going to read a number forwards, and when I stop, I want you to say that number backwards."

A normal person of average intelligence makes one error or none, and a person with a functioning IQ of 110, or college level, makes none. In the presence of anxiety, many test performances, including those on this test, are diminished, and the examiner must overcome some of this anxiety to obtain adequate results.

In the presence of a moderate brain syndrome, three or four errors are made in the course of the serial subtractions.

Example: (99) 92, 85, 78,
61, 56, 37, 30, 23, 15, 8, *1*

3. *Digit Span Backwards*

The "Digit Span Backwards" is a simple test to administer and to score, using a table of digits from the Wechsler tests or the Wells manual. The score consists of the total of digits retained on two successive trials.

A person without a brain syndrome, and of normal intelligence can retain 7 digits forward (as in a telephone number) and can retain 6 or 5 digits backwards. At a lower level of IQ functioning, that of 50-70, or the moron level, an individual without a brain syndrome can retain 5 or 4 digits backward. Retention of less than this number of digits is found in brain syndromes of various causes.

Many persons with an IQ below 70, either with or without the brain syndrome, have difficulty in formulating what is demanded of them so that it is necessary to instruct the patient in making such a reversal, using numbers which will not appear in the test.

   4. Picture Absurdities

   Simple pictures in which an absurdity is present (such a picture of a signpost with its shadow on the sun side of the post) comprise a simple test of abstract judgement. The subject must be able to perceive and conceive the absurdity, but to express his observations, need not be fluent in the language of the examiner. Thus illiterates and persons from whom the examiner is separated by a language barrier may become easily testable by this technique.

   After saying that "There is something wrong with each one of these pictures," the examiner points to each one, asking, "What is wrong with this? This test and the following picture tests are presented in useful form in a pocket size book, the *Mental Examiners' Handbook,* by F. L. Wells, Ph.D., and Jurgen Ruesch, M.D., published by the Psychological Corporation of New York. This publication is available to qualified psychologists.

   In my experience, persons with an IQ of 50 or above who do not have a brain syndrome, can recognize 5 out of 5 of these picture absurdities. Persons with a brain syndrome make errors.

   A technical note of importance to the medical examiner concerns the acuity of visual perception in this test. For older persons and for others whose vision will be improved by a positive lens, I carry in my kit a pair of spectacles with +3 sphere lenses. These are equivalent to mail order reading glasses for older people. The use of these spectacles facilitates rapport and examination.

   5. Visual Retention

   This also requires a prepared and standardized set of pictures. In the manual by Wells and Ruesch which is noted above, this set consists of pages which each show 10 common objects—a shoe, a necklace, a paint can, etc. The examiner points to each object, saying, "What is this?" After obtaining a response on each item, he immediately closes the book and asks the subject to name the objects. Persons with an IQ above 50 retain at least 7 of the 10 objects. Persons with brain syndromes retain fewer than 7 or 6, and often have difficulty with retaining more than 3 or 2.

5. *Picture Similarities*

Also relying on pictures for a test of the ability to abstract the similarity from a series of different objects is the Wells-Reusch test of Picture Similarities. The examiner displays a page which depicts 10 objects, one page, for example, showing fruit and vegetables, and asks, "In what way are these alike?" An "abstract" answer, for example, an answer that indicates the edibility or the vegetable kingdom nature which they have in common, is a normal answer, unless they show the signs of a thinking disorder such as Schizophrenia, or a brain syndrome.

This test is cognate to the demonstration item in the Similarities subtest of the Wechsler Adult Intelligence Scale. In the Wechsler subtest, the examiner asks, "In what way are an orange and a banana alike?" The full answer is, "They are both fruit, they have skins, and can be eaten." In the picture test, however, the order of abstraction is lower, and the level of communication between examiner and examinee need not be so high.

Affect in the Brain Syndrome

An individual in whom a brain syndrome is developing, senses the increasing limitation of his capacities which this syndrome produces, often without being able consciously to perceive the details of his defects, and sometimes being unwilling to admit them. Confronted by this nameless adversary which causes an ingravescent decline in his abilities, the individual often reacts by becoming depressed. This depression can be generally mild and short lasting. In a group of senescent institutionalized persons, such reactions lasted no longer than one or two days, responding promptly to a minimal display of human contact, affection or love.

But in individuals who have had an excessive need for love through their younger years, or an ungratifiable or obsessive need, the sense of increasing incapacity which is produced by the brain syndrome is threatening. Added to the individual's personal predisposition to depression, the brain syndrome adds its precipitating depressing effect, producing a depressive state that may be sufficiently severe to merit specialized care. Thus when the general physician or psychiatrist encounters a middle aged patient who is depressed, but in whom he can find no specific event that seems competent to precipitate the depression, he must promptly search for a brain syndrome, which may be the exciting cause of the depression.

Such a chronic depression is related to the phenomenon of "disengagement" as described by Henry Cummings (48). In disengagement, the aging individual recognizes or perceives some decline in his perceptual abilities, leading to his becoming more clearly aware of the inevitability of his death, and disengages quanta of his energies, in anticipation of dying. These depressive psychological reactions of the person with a brain syndrome, it should again be noted, are superadded to the physical brain damage which he has suffered. This combination can be a formidable one in some individuals, resulting in the remarkably high rate of suicide in senescents (see page 63).

Other changes in affect take place as a concomitant of the brain syndrome. These are mainly based on the individual's previous characterological development, and can be understood by learning the details of his personality in his younger years, for they are seen to be exaggerations of his previous affectual pattern. Thus the "old soldier becomes more soldierly, and the pedant more pedantic" (15).

Behavior in the Brain Syndrome

Following an injury to the principal organ of adaptation, the brain, the behavior tends to become maladaptive. Such maladaptation accounts in part for the high rate of automotive fatalities among the elderly. Also related is the fact that a sudden and unexpected behavior by an older person may have its basis in a brain syndrome.

A 60-year-old man who seemed to be in good health, who had driven his automobile satisfactorily in the past, was driving in the left hand lane as he approached a stoplight. Suddenly he swerved at undiminished speed into the right hand lane, causing injuries to two persons, as well as some property damage. Examination showed a mild brain syndrome which did not improve, although no cause was found at first. Further examination proved that a cancer of the lung, which was too small for early detection, had nevertheless spread to the brain.

As described earlier in the section on Senescence, one of the less well understood behaviors of the elderly is in the sexual area. This lack of understanding contributes to the fact that most of the crimes of the elderly are sex crimes.

Other behavioral phenomena, which more often appear in a medical history, are seizures and incontinence. Convulsive or non-convulsive seizure attacks are often a feature of a brain syndrome and assist diagnosis and treatment. Incontinence of urine, for example, appears more often in disease of the frontal lobe than of the parietal lobe (15, p. 379).

Prognosis in the Brain Syndrome

Finally, what of the prognosis in different forms of the brain syndrome? An intensive study on this subject was conducted, (37) on 117 men and women who were examined while in-patients at a large general hospital, the 117 composing 16 percent of in-patient psychiatric consultations at this hospital during a 4-year period. Within 5 years of the beginning of this study, one-half of the brain syndrome patients had died. Seventeen percent of the total number of patients died during their hospital stay.

Twelve percent required psychiatric hospitalization. One-quarter of this group also died, and one-half of those who were admitted to psychiatric hospitals required long term psychiatric hospitalization. Of the 31 patients who were alive and able to be interviewed at the end of the five-year study, more than one-half showed a significant dementia.

The autopsies which were done revealed the expected incidence of vascular disease of the brain and heart, and of metastatic cancer, but also an unexpectedly high incidence of renal disease and uremia. The onset of a severe chronic brain syndrome in the course of a medical illness is thus a grave sign.

CHAPTER 5

NORMALCY

THE MORAL NORMAL

The concept of the normal man, or of normalcy itself, is one which has stimulated students, scholars and expositors to offer so many discrepant definitions of this subject that we shall begin by giving a definition of what normalcy is not: Normalcy is not a moral image of one's personal, individual concept of the normal man. And normalcy is not a value judgement which is based on a subjective, idiosyncratic scheme of values. Normalcy is not a quality which is found exclusively on the laudable side of the dichotomy between good and bad, right and wrong, Divine and human, familiar and strange, or Greeks and barbarians.

Yet we frequently allow ourselves to render moral judgements, whether we be the mighty or the meek. Here in testimony before the United States Senate, an accomplished criminal defense lawyer and currently a district attorney (40) delivered himself in populist language of his feelings on juvenile delinquency:

> "Well, what has happened to this great country? . . . Senator, you will agree with me, and every right thinking man that is not a fool will agree, that there has been a deterioration of the moral climate in our country. You see it all over. The old things that were tried and true when you were a kid and I was a kid, that is all gone by the board. If it is old, it is dirty; if it is old and tried and true, it has to be discarded."

And here a warden of a large penitentiary, who refuses to traffic in the gray zone between black and white, pronounces his presumptions from a platform which is totally unencumbered by research into the facts of the matter (16):

"Narcotics users almost invariably are victims of sex frustrations. They're inadequate, or clumsy, or sexually small. Often, they are the object of ridicule because of their failure to complete the sex act. So they turn to dope and become addicted. It reduces their sex drive, and they seem to be happy in their own little world of fantasy. Sex no longer means very much to them, but of course they're still in trouble because they have swapped a bad problem for a worse one. Drug addicts almost never get involved in direct sex crimes, although they are often picked up for pandering. The crimes they commit are more likely to be robbery, blackmail or peddling, because they'll do anything to raise money for the support of their habit."

And even our legislation is shaped by the wind of moralizing. In a decision by a U.S. District Court, Judge Craver cited a statute that was enacted into law in 1869, which was still effective at the time of a key case in 1964 (Perkins v. State of North Carolina). The North Carolina General Statute § 14-177 reads:

"If any person shall commit the abominable and detestable crime against nature, with mankind or beast, he shall be imprisoned in the State's prison for not less than five, nor more than sixty years."

This item is rather empathetic, however, when it is compared to the statute which it replaced. The North Carolina statute of 1837 reads:

"Any person who shall commit the abominable and detestable crime against nature, not to be named among Christians, with either mankind or beast, shall be adjudged guilty of a felony and shall suffer death with benefit of clergy."

But the 1837 statute in our young republic which had been founded on the separation of church and state, was itself derived from an edict which was issued by Henry VIII in 1533:

"Any person who shall commit the abominable and detestable vice of buggery with either mankind or beast, shall be adjudged guilty of a felony and shall suffer death without the benefit of clergy."

Readers of a calendrical frame of mind will recall that Henry VIII created this law during the period between his being awarded the title of "Defender of the Faith" by the Pope, and his excommunication, but previous to his execution of his chancellors Thomas More and Thomas Cromwell, and of his wives Anne Boleyn and Catherine Howard, among many others. Since that period, the concept of "abominable" has altered somewhat.

So pervasive is this moral image of normalcy that even specialists in the mental health sciences have joined the chorus. A popular psychiatric writer demonstrated the confusion of subjective moral values with objective psychological and behavioral data. This doctor (66) first proposed that mental normalcy is equivalent to mental health and then continued:

> "Let us define mental health as the adjustment of human beings to the world and to each other with a maximum of effectiveness and happiness. Not just efficiency, or just contentment, or the grace of obeying the rules of the game cheerfully. It is all of these together. It is the ability to maintain an even temper, an alert intelligence, socially considerate behavior, and a happy disposition. This, I think is a healthy mind."

But not all subjectivity on the topic of normalcy is both as moralizing as we see in the above example, and also as sermonic in its tone. Grinker (35), in a study of students who were training at a small Christian college to become teachers of physical education, first shared with his readers his personal shock at the encounter. "The impact of these interviews was startling! Here was a type of young man I had not met before in my role as a psychiatrist, and rarely in my personal life." Reeling from the appulsion, he wrote that he was reassured by a previous observer's statement that an analyst who was confronted by a normal man "would be struck dumb, for once, through lack of appropriate ideas." (To the author of this book, who has known a good many psychoanalysts, the possibility of such an analyst being made temporarily speechless, or stricken dumb for lack of appropriate ideas, seems a rare happening indeed.)

But then the same writer demonstrates a variety of subjectivity which at first flirts with moralizing, and later becomes its bedfellow. In explaining the title of his paper, "Mentally Healthy Young Males (Homoclites), he wrote:

> "Because such terms as "normal" and "healthy" are so heavily loaded with value judgments, a neutral word was sought but not

found in the English language. Even the Greeks did not have a word for the condition I am describing. Dr. Percival Bailey made the suggestion that, since heteroclite means a person deviating from the common rule, the opposite or 'homoclite' would designate a person following the common rule. The reader will soon discover that the population to be described is composed of 'normal,' 'healthy,' 'ordinary,' 'just plain guys,' in fact homoclites!''

Here we have a well-informed representative from the school of hopeful hedonism, who quite subtly invokes the moral values of happiness (73) that is achieved through passivity:

"The small proportion of the number of deviants in any culture is not a function of the same instinct with which that society has built itself upon the fundamental societies, but the universal fact that, happily, the majority of mankind quite readily take any shape that is presented to them."

Moralizing has its psychological purposes, with which the practicing psychiatrist or psychologist is familiar. One of the psychodynamic uses to which moral judgements are put is their use to deny an individual's prohibited strivings, which on psychological study are seen to be that individual's "immoral" urges.

A recent case which illustrates this point is that of a 55-year-old executive, who closed most psychotherapeutic attempts to learn his feelings or reactions by saying, "Well . . . it was normal . . . I guess." This patient, who had been referred by his family physician for marriage counselling, complained that his wife had a single sexual experience with his twin sister's husband. The alleged episode, which was simply and dispassionately negated by the wife, was said to have taken place when both of the affected spouses were out of the home, and the patient had been telephoning home approximately every hour "to see if he were needed at home." He felt that he was sure of this sexual activity having been performed because of a look on his wife's face which was not easy to define except that it was not "normal," and also that his brother-in-law had once boasted about some extramarital conquests. More significant to him, to establish in his mind that he had been given a cuckolding, was the fact that his wife had become *more* sexually responsive to him. However, at about the time of the episode, he had consulted a urologist because of a disorder of the prostate gland, and acting on his interpretation of the urologist's advice, began having intercourse with his wife every night, "to drain out the gland." But he also did not notice any change in his wife's responsiveness when, much later, he took the therapist's advice to perform intercourse within the vagina, instead of by using premature withdrawal, which had been this couple's practice for 25 years.

He also admitted that people look at him more closely than at others, and that he feels shy about expressing himself, but that this was "... normal, I guess." Yet he failed to put the postscript of normal on a most scant description of his early life with his twin sister, who was his only sibling. Much later, we learned that he had prohibited sexual fantasies about his sister, and that his brother-in-law represented an individual who had the moral sanction to act out these fantasies.

"... normal" meant to the patient and therapist in this context that "it was not prohibited," or "I was not immoral."

Thus the term normal can be used either openly or covertly by citizens who are concerned with law or psychology, as a subjective moral value judgment, or it can be used by any of us as a psychological defense against such a value judgment.

But what is objective normalcy?

THE HEALTHY NORMAL

The second concept of normalcy, which like the first is covered with the fine patina of acceptability, is that normalcy is health. Health is usually defined as the absence of disease. But most definitions of disease state that disease, itself, is the absence of health, which leaves us in a difficult position, but nevertheless the same position as the American Medical Association. In that Association's Journal (47), a "disease" is defined as follows:

"In general, any deviation from a state of health; an illness or a sickness; more specifically, a definite morbid process having a characteristic train of symptoms. It may affect the whole body or any of its parts, and its etiology, pathology or prognosis may be known or unknown."

In medical practice, the concrete description of specific diseases, with their characteristic train of symptoms, is rather firmly based on generally accepted diagnostic criteria. Thus in general medicine, various committees of specialists have developed diagnostic guide-lines in the *International Classification of Disease* and in psychiatry, a similar select committee has produced the *Diagnostic and Statistical Manual of Mental Disorders* (4) which together set forth the positive characteristics of most disease syndromes. With these uniform criteria before him, the medical or psychiatric clinician is able to subject an individual to increasingly fine screening in the search for disease patterns. If the search yields negative results, the diagnosis is made of "no disease." This diagnosis of no disease carries with it the presumption of health, which by our current hypothesis, is normalcy.

> "As doctors, we see any major deviation from the norm as unhealthy; and therefore, any such deviation is ill-health or sickness. Thus, in our book we include as mental disorders such deviations as learning difficulties, stress reactions, sexual deviations, mental deficiency, antisocial behavior. By book, I mean the volume called *Diagnostic and Statistical Manual of Mental Disorders,* published by this Association (American Psychiatric Association). Now mark this well—It is going to haunt us. This is a list of mental disorders. It says so on the cover. Therefore, "transient situational disturbances"—so listed—must be mental disorders; so are alcoholism, habit disturbances, dyssocial reaction, conduct disturbances, mental deficiencies, speech disturbances, and so on . . .
> "Therefore, these deviations are illnesses. Our categories are so broad that we would squeeze into them such concepts as hostility to an employer, or marital discord over money" (Davidson, 1958).

These medical diagnoses usually estimate the efficiency of functioning of the individual's organ or system which is diagnosed. In cardiology, for example, the efficiency of the heart as a pump is given as part of the diagnosis. Similarly, if impairment of the heart's function is found, as in various forms of heart failure, then it is assumed that there is some disease of the heart. Using the criterion of impairment, then, if there is impairment, which implies that there is disease, abnormality exists; while if there is no impairment, and therefore no disease, there will be health, hence normalcy.

A major study in mental health which posits certain of the above assumptions will be summarized here in order to help us predict how often we may encounter the unimpaired, or healthy, normal individual. At the College of Medicine of Cornell University, in New York, Srole and his associates (85) formed a team of investigators which consisted of psychiatrists, psychologists, social workers, social scientists and statisticians, under the leadership of the chairman of the department of Social Psychiatry, Thomas A.C. Rennie, M.D.

These investigators chose as their sample a group of 175,000 men and women, aged 20-59 years of age, who lived in the midtown section of New York, entitling their first report the "Midtown Study" (85). This sample is generally representative of the urban United States except for a few items: the ratio of women to men in Midtown was 125 to 100, compared to the U.S. ratio of about 104 women to 100 men. Wives who were working at full time or part time jobs in Midtown comprised 53% of the sample, compared to 26% among the white urban wives throughout the country. Children under age 15 comprised only 15% of the population that was reviewed in Midtown, while 28% of the general American population was under age 15. However, observers felt that these discrepancies did not at all vitiate the results which were reported.

The investigators proposed, tested and published their criteria for making a diagnosis of impairment of function due to mental illness, and a classification of the severity of this impairment. In this classification, individuals were placed in one of six categories, consisting of Well, Mild Impairment, Moderate Impairment, Marked Impairment, Severe Impairment, or Incapacitating Impairment.

Of the 175,000 persons in the sample, 1911 were chosen as representative, and 1660 were interviewed at their homes. The interviews were carried out by two skilled social workers who had worked closely with the other professional members of the team, on standards and techniques. Their findings were highly significant (Table 1).

The criteria by which these investigators classified their subjects as Well or having different grades of impairment are deserving of description and example. The judgment of Well was not given if the subject responded either "often," or "nearly all the time" (as opposed to "sometimes"), to the questions, "Is your stomach upset?" or "Do you have cold sweats?", or "Does your heart beat hard?" Similarly, the judgment of Well was not given if the subject responded "yes" to the questions covering whether they have "Such restlessness I can't sit long in a chair," or "Periods of days, weeks, months when I couldn't get going," or "Always be on guard against people," or "Feel people are against me" (p. 396).

The two psychiatrists who served as judges for this study

Table 1. Mental Impairment in the Community.
Less than one-fifth of the population was well.

MIDTOWN STUDY

Degree of Mental Impairment		Percent	Subtotal
None	"The Well Group"	18.5	
Mild		36.3	
Moderate		21.8	58.1
Marked		13.2	
Severe	"The Impaired Group"	7.5	23.4
Incapacitated		2.7	

differed only slightly in their assessment of impairment, as can be seen from the summaries which they offered in their study, *Mental Health in the Metropolis* (p. 402).

Thus, of this group of individuals who were interviewed at home, the authors write, "Compressed into a single sentence, the subclinical forms of symptom formation aggregate almost a 60% majority of the sample adults, and on the other side of this modal group are the sample of Well individuals, and the segment of Impaired people, each representing somewhat more than 20% of this sample."

We have described this sample from Midtown, in which a total of 18.5% were well, or normal by our current definition, as having been at home. What of those residents of Midtown who were not at home? At the same time this sample was being studied, a survey was made of Midtown individuals (57) also aged 20-59 years who required mental hospitalization. Individuals who had been in mental hospitals for five years or more (five years is the period of time required in a New York statute that describes "incurable insanity") numbered over 500 persons per 100,000 of the population. Projected onto a United States population of 200 million, this represents one million chronic mental inpatients, who at the present state of the science and art of psychiatry, will be hospitalized for much of their lives. In our population, therefore, the number of well persons, or "healthy normal" individuals, is shrinking.

The authors of the above study estimated that their observations on the number of Well persons were too high, and the number of people with mental impairments were estimated at too low a level. This tendency toward underestimation of impairment becomes more significant in the older group.

> The number of older persons is growing, both in the total number of older individuals, and in the increase in their relative number as well. This number of persons who is 65 years of age or older in the U.S., has grown from 3.1 million in 1900, to some 18 million in 1965. In 1900, 1 person in 25 was 65 years of age or older. In 1965, 1 of 11 persons in the U.S. was in this age group. By 1975, this ratio will probably be 1 to 9, and this proportion is already found in many of our states and cities.

In this burgeoning older population, what is the proportion of normal individuals? If normalcy requires that the individual be mentally healthy, this is small:

> "In one metropolitan community survey, 11.5 per cent of persons aged 65 or over were found to be mentally ill. Almost 3 per cent were said to be suffering from psychosis, and about 7 per cent from psychoneurosis. These estimates are probably low.
>
> In another household survey of persons 65 years of age or over, it was found that 6.3 per cent were so disordered mentally that they met clinical criteria for involuntary mental hospital admission. These people showed a rising proportion of mental illness with age, starting at 3.2 per cent in the 65-69 age group and increasing to 9.5 per cent in the 80-84 age group. More than 30 per cent of those over 85 years of age who were interviewed were found to meet the clinical criteria for involuntary certification to mental hospitals. In all age groups, the proportion of the mentally ill was greater among men than among women. These estimates may be low; a number of persons who were believed to be confused were kept from the survey interviewers by relatives.
>
> Other studies indicate that from 10 to 20 per cent of persons over 65 in the community have a significant degree of memory defect, disorientation, and decline in intellectual performance" (36).

The older age group and the adult sector have been reviewed for their number of non-healthy or abnormal individuals, but we have not yet reported on the younger age group. To summarize many of the expert professional investigations on mental illness among young people, we shall simply quote from an Associated Press dispatch of October 25, 1969:

"Almost 10 million Americans under 25 years of age need help from mental health workers, but most are not getting it, a special study group has informed Congress.

The Joint Committee on the Mental Health of Children, calling for a drive against a 'national tragedy', estimated an ultimate cost of $6 billion to $10 billion a year."

In the eyes of this committee, then, out of 95 million Americans who are under the age of 25, about 10 per cent are in need of active mental health care. Thus the younger group as well as the adult and the older groups are all characterized by the fact that mental health or mental wellness is the exception, rather than the rule.

PHYSICAL NORMALCY

So far in our search for the healthy normal individual, we have examined the mental health of the community's citizens, to find that less than one fifth of the community is mentally healthy or mentally normal. Is the picture of our physcial health an equally poor one? To examine this question, let us first see the figures on the causes of death, and then those on the illnesses which are due to physical disease.

In the following table (Table 2), we have listed the death rates that are produced by the twelve most common causes of death. (Reported accidents, suicide and homicide are presented here in their order among the leading causes of death, without discussing the close relationship between the mental factors and the physical factors which are involved in these three causes of fatality). Looking over these statistics for a recent year, we see that almost two per cent of the total population died in that year, and that the three most common causes of death were heart disease, cancer and stroke. Many of the causes of death consisted of conditions that are chronic, such as most of the cases of heart disease, cancer or stroke. In addition to those who die from these causes, we should therefore expect a larger number of persons to be ill, or disabled because of these conditions. That this is true, is well demonstrated.

A household survey, based on 42,000 homes that represented

134,000 persons (97), gives an estimate of chronic disease or chronic impairment that is due to selected physical disorders.

"An estimated 93.7 million persons, or 49.1 percent of the civilian, noninstitutional population of the United States had one or more chronic diseases or impairments during July 1965-June 1966. Among the persons with chronic conditions about 21.4 million had some degree of limitation of activity and 6.1 million had some form of mobility limitation, and an estimated 5.8 million persons had both limited activity and mobility. These estimates are based on information collected in household interviews by the Health Interview Survey during the 12 months ending with June 1966. Since the population surveyed excludes members of the Armed Forces and persons confined in institutions, the estimates shown in this report are an undercount of the total number of limited persons in the United States."

Table 2. Death Rates

DEATH RATES IN THE U.S.

(DEATHS FROM THE MOST COMMON CAUSES)

Cause	Death Rate (per 100,000 population)
Heart Disease	364.5
Cancer and malignancies	157.2
Stroke	102.2
Generalized Artery Disease	19.0
Circulatory Disease not listed above	15.1
Diabetes	17.7
Early infancy Disorders	24.4
Influenza and Pneumonia	28.8
Other Broncho pulmonary disease	14.8
Accidents	57.2
Suicide	10.8
Homicide	6.8

Death rates in the United States for 1967, from the *Vital Statistics of the U.S.* by the Department of Health, Education and Welfare, the U.S. Public Health Service. Total reported deaths for 1967 — 1,851,322.

This is a mortality figure. The figures for morbidity, or illness, will be given in the next table.

The conditions that are enumerated in the above report are Arthritis and Rheumatism, Hypertension without heart involvement, Heart conditions, Peptic ulcer, Diseases of thyroid gland, Hernia, Diabetes, Malignant neoplasm, Disease of the gall bladder, and Vascular lesions of the nervous system. The definition of chronic was made to mean that the condition was present for three months or more. It was pointed out that these figures represent an undercount of the total amount of illness (or morbidity) in the community because of the sampling technique. It should also be noted that these figures include only chronic limitations, so that acute illnesses and injuries increase the number of those on the imparied list.

As one would expect, the incidence of these disabling illnesses rises with age (97). In persons under 17, only about 22% show chronic disease conditions, but many more than half of all persons over 17 show one or more chronic disease conditions. Table 3 shows this rapid increase of chronic disorders as the population ages.

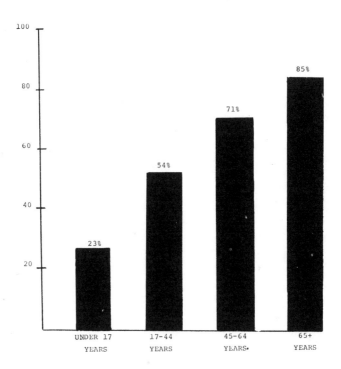

Hence our search for the "healthy normal" man comes to a conclusion. If we say that the normal person is a healthy person, who is not impaired by mental or physcial disease, we shall have to search with ardor and dedication in order to find such persons in large numbers. Impairment which is due to mental illness is present in over 80% of the population, and impairment which is due to chronic and acute physical illnesses and injuries, is found in over 50% of the population. The healthy normal man is thus a fictional character, even though he is an ideal fiction.

THE MODAL NORMAL

The oldest, and until recently the most acceptable definition of the normal, is that the normal is the average. This fiction has been supported by the work of mathematical logicians who propose that an individual whose description falls between the shoulders of a bell-shaped curve of distribution, or a normal curve, is a normal individual.

The following narrative description of this normal curve, which is familiar to students of the history of science, will define the key terms that follow. The German mathematician, Gauss, is said to have visited the North Sea around 1807, immediately after a storm had cast up an unusually large number of herring on the beach. Gauss promptly produced the brass compass and rule which he invariably carried, to measure all the herring in one hectare. He found that most of the specimens were 15 centimeters in length, and that a lesser number were either 16 or 14 centimeters, and that a still lesser number were 17 or 13 centimeters, and so on. This observation supported his mathematical theory of error, for which he is well known.

A graph of these measurements takes the form of a typical bell shaped curve. The shoulders of the curve, mentioned above, are the points at which the numbers begin to fall off rapidly. This bell shaped curve is called a normal curve.

> "Technically, normal is a term which describes a particular kind of mathematical graph and statistical phenomenon. If certain measurements are made of a very large number of individuals, for example, and half below a certain point, with most falling very close to it, and diminishing numbers falling further and further from that point in

precisely equal proportions on both sides of it, then the entire array
is called a normal distribution (73).

On any such curve, or on any coherent series of measurements,
there are three points that are of value to us in understanding the
mathematical description of the modal man. These are the mode,
the median and the mean. The mode is the measurement or the
observation which occurs most often, the median is the measurement which is chosen so that there are as many above as there are
below, and the mean is the intermediate between two extremes. It
is the "modal man" or that manner of man which occurs most
often on the curve we have currently chosen, who is most often
considered the normal man. The average, which is nearer to the
mean than to the mode, is also frequently conceived of as normal.

An example of this concept was given by Quetelet, the Belgian
statistician, who around 1846 is credited with making the first
application of Gauss' curve of error to human individuals. Quetelet
wrote, with Aristotlean moralism, that the average man appears as
nature's ideal, so that deviations toward the good side, or deviations toward the bad, are the result of nature's errors in its
attempt to create an ideal.

It is this historical substrate of the modal as the normal man
that has played a role in the development of the word "normal."
This word is derived from the root which yielded the Latin norma,
which means a carpenter's square, or a mason's square (which are
right angles, and not full squares), so that normal means according
to rule, or following the principle.

But the curves on which human data can be plotted are not
normal curves, as defined above, but are abnormal. For example,
the measurement of human intelligence does not yield a normal
Gaussian curve, but is skewed to the left, on the side in which
lower intelligence quotients are located. This is familiar to psychologists, who report that in almost every population there are
more idiots and imbeciles than there are geniuses.

But when we go beyond the study of one factor such as the
intelligence quotient as estimated by one particular test instru-
ment, to the study of multiple factors which operate in human
biology, psychology and sociology, we find that very few of us
pass the tests that would admit us to the status of being the modal
man.

A witty British pathologist, writing for other physicians on "The Normal Range," agrees in this manner.

"The solution proposed by [another doctor] of using a large sample of carefully screened healthy persons, represents a lapse into subjectivism ... I presume that by "healthy" they mean free from dental caries, alopecia, sinusitis, presbyopia, myopia, reduced auditory acuity, diminished forced expiratory volume, neurosis, allergy, etc. which rules out anyone over the age of 20 years. If they include immaturity, that excludes anyone under the age of 20 years. And if they also include possible heterozygotes for known diseases, that eliminates the whole of mankind several times over (78)."

An experimental physiologist (73) writes:

"If we imagine the human population to consist of individuals who are in the average range with respect to the various items which enter into their make-up, we are misleading ourselves to such a degree that sound human understanding is impossible. . . .

It may surprise the reader to know that there is only about one chance in 6,500 that he individually has a medium size stomach, a heart with medium pumping capacity, a thyroid gland of medium activity, a medium number of islets of Langerhans in his pancreas, a medium calcium requirement and a medium vitamin A requirement. If we make the number of categories larger, and even if we enlarge the median group to include much more than the middle one-third, the chance that any individual will be in the median group in all respects is so small as to be negligible.

The existence in every human being of a vast array of attributes which are potentially measurable (whether by present methods or not), and probably often uncorrelated mathematically, makes quite tenable the hypothesis that *practically every human being is a deviate in some respects.*"

Thus the modal or statistical normal is a construct which is applicable to a single set of simple observations, but when it is applied to the complexities of human life, is unmasked as a mathematical fiction. For man is more than a biological beast who is regulated by a single physiological force. He also has his psychological aspect, containing a great number of diverse trends, and his sociological side, with its great variety of fluctuating field forces. For when we colligate the many different factors which we describe in man under the heading of his body, his mind and his character, we conclude that there is no modal normal man.

THE TELEVISION MODE

The mode in television programs for children has been examined and reported on in hearings before the United States Senate (84). Television programs during the "children's hours" of 4:00 p.m. to 9:00 p.m., Monday through Friday, were studied for acts of violence. In these programs, a rough division was made between "humorous" acts of violence, if they were a part of cartoons or comedy, and "non-humorous" acts of violence.

"In a sample of 100 non-humorous children's hours the following were observed:

12 murders.

16 major gunfights

21 persons shot (apparently not fatally).

21 other violent incidents with guns (ranging from shooting at the missing persons, to shooting up a town).

37 hand-to-hand fights (15 fist fights, 15 incidents in which one person slugged another, an attempted murder with a pitchfork, 2 stranglings, a fight in the water, a case in which a woman was gagged and tied to a bed, and so forth).

1 stabbing in the back with a butcher knife.

4 attempted suicides, three successful.

4 people falling or pushed over cliffs.

2 cars running over cliffs

2 attempts made in automobiles to run over persons on the sidewalk

A psychotic loose and raving in a flying airliner.

2 mob scenes, in one of which the mob hangs the wrong man

A horse grinding a man under its hooves.

A great deal of miscellaneous violence, including a plane fight, a hired killer stalking his prey, 2 robberies, a pickpocket working, a woman killed by falling from a train, a tidal wave, an earthquake, and a guillotining.

This is modal, but is it normal?

THE CHRONOLOGICAL MODAL NORMAL

When we observe a single individual's life history, we see that each stage of development between birth and death has a style of its own, in which the individual's mode of life is affected by his stage in life. The mode of behavior which we can expect of an infant, for example, would be grossly inacceptable in an adult. The expression of this expectation is generally credited to Diderot in his statement that "were a three year old to be endowed with the intellectual and physical strength of an adult, he would be a monster."

> A boy of four who had an imaginary playmate was walking along the beach with his father, who was holding his hand. The boy said, "Daddy, I'm taller than you."
> He gave up the imaginary playmate sometime after his fifth birthday, and by the age of seventeen, was, indeed, taller than his father. At the age of 23, he was considered somewhat more persistent than others, and had acquired much more physical strength than the average. His development and status were considered by lay and professional observers to be normal.
> But for him, at the age of 23, to consider himself taller than a man whose height was objectively greater, would be considered abnormal. Observers would believe that he had made a slip of speech, or had expressed an illusion, a delusion or hallucination.

In adolescence, Erikson, who is one of our most perceptive students of this period, believes that a phase of identity crisis is a normal developmental phenomenon. Identity, as he uses it, is roughly equivalent to what we have described as the ego. (A clinical case of identity crisis, with a pathological outcome, is described in the first chapter.) But for an adult to experience such a crisis and then to be defeated by it, would stimulate observers to search for the signs of schizophrenia, a syndrome which until 1911 was known as *dementia praecox,* or insanity of the adolescent.

Erikson describes most clearly the significant needs of the individual at different phases in his development, putting these needs in a chronological order that consists of eight steps. These steps, or the "Eight Ages of Man" (17) begin with four periods which are essentially the same as Freud's early developmental phases, but then go on through adolescence to old age. During each chronological age, Erikson shows that there is a pair of significant characteristics of the personality, of which each part competes with the other for dominance, and then for incorporation into the personality. The successful member of each pair, accompanied to a smaller extent by relics of its opposite member, becomes a trait of the maturing personality, with the later traits becoming dynamically added to the earlier.

Table 4. Erikson's Eight Ages of Man

Age	Developmental Phase	Competing Personality Traits
1	Oral	Trust — Mistrust
2-3	Anal	Autonomy — Doubt
4-5	Phallic	Initiative — Guilt
6-11	Latency	Industry — Inferiority
12-18	Adolescence	Ego Identity — Role Confusion
19-50	Young Adult	Intimacy — Isolation
51-64	Middle Age	Generativity — Self Absorption
65-	'Old' Age	Integrity — Despair

Each developmental phase, above, represents a period in the individual's life during which that individual has a propensity to develop either a personality trait, or the opposite of that personality trait.

The initial four developmental phases are those proposed by Freud (1905) and are generally accepted by most psychologists and psychiatrists. All ages are approximate.

Thus the needs of the individual at different phases promote the rise of a characterological trait which is specific for that phase. This in turn supports our conception that it is "normal" to react to certain inner psychological needs by means of developing specific characteristics of the personality which vary during the chronology of the individual, from the cradle to the grave.

THE CULTURAL NORMAL

At any time in the history of a culture, various beliefs and behaviors fall within the limits of the acceptable normal for that culture, while they are not acceptable to nearby cultures. As an example, some of the Indians of the Southwestern United States believe in the supernatural and also in witchcraft, at the same time that they do not believe in the scientific determinism which states that an ostensible cause produces an observable effect. Thus a Hopi who should slip on the ice and break a leg, may believe that the fall which precipitated his fracture was not a somatopsychic event, as would his Caucasian neighbors, but rather the result of action that was taken by some spirit.

An Apache tribal member whose family name was Wolf and who belonged to the Native American Church had participated in a religious service which included the ingestion of peyote, which contains mescaline, a powerful hallucinogenic drug. The use of this drug for such purposes is sanctioned by the church and is not prohibited by the federal government. However, this Wolf had a "bad trip" in that his psychotic reaction to the drug persisted longer than expected, and took an impermissible direction.

He believed that he actually was a wolf, and began to snarl and bite people, while moving about on all fours. Since he did this during a winter snow, at an elevation of 8000 feet without wearing shoes or gloves, he developed four frostbitten extremities, which became black with gangrene. Both the Caucasian doctor who treated him and many of his tribe felt that the frostbite was abnormal, but that the wolflike behavior was culturally normal.

An act may be morally wrong, or legally wrong in one culture, and yet the same act may be permissible in another culture which coexists in adjoining territory. Such a history evolved on an Indian reservation in Arizona.

An Apache man of about 70, who was known to have become somewhat forgetful and enfeebled, took his wife to a witch for treatment of her eye troubles. The witch administered a potion, and charged a fee, and the wife improved. However, in a few months, the eye troubles returned. This time the witch administered a much more powerful potion, it was stated, and charged ten times the previous fee. Again, after a few months the symptoms recurred.

The husband reasoned that since the witch could cure the affliction, the witch could also produce the affliction. Worse yet, the husband felt that the witch actually caused the symptoms to reappear in order to earn another fee. He then produced a handgun with which he shot and killed the witch. An officer of the tribal justice system decreed that this behavior was expectably normal. On the other hand, the U.S. Federal Court, which has jurisdiction in cases of major crime on the Indian reservation, could well have taken another view (7).

THE PSYCHOADAPTIVE NORMAL

Our previous definitions of normalcy could well have been made by a specialist in sociology or in preventive medicine, for they focus, as do those disciplines, on the interaction of the individual with his environment. But to the psychologist and the psychiatrist, who concentrate on the feelings and thinking which determine the behavior of an individual, it becomes possible to define the normalcy of an individual by observing that individual's personal psychological processes. Many psychologists state that an essential feature of normalcy is that the individual's psychological processes demonstrate the phenomenon of functional adaptation. In addition to functional adaptation as a general requirement of normalcy, they particularly state that the normal man adapts his subjective strivings, which are emotional and prelogical, to the world of reality, which is objectively logical.

The term adaptation is used here in the sense which was developed by Darwin, to mean the enhancement of the individual over a prolonged period of time, as a reaction to many stresses that arise from the environment. Along these lines, the World Committee on Mental Health suggested that mental health, and in this case normalcy, is a condition

> "which enables the individual to achieve a satisfactory synthesis of his potentially conflicting instinctive drives; to form and maintain harmonious relations with others; and to participate in constructive changes in his social and physical environment."

Masserman, a highly original scholar, takes essentially the same position by defining normal conduct as "more effectively and lastingly adaptive."

The adaptational feature of normalcy is heavily emphasized by Klein (53) as a part of "character strength." In a lengthy essay, Klein writes that normalcy requires a successful integration of five adaptive elements of the personality.

> *1. Emotional Maturity.* The adult who is emotionally mature will counter his sensing a lack of gratification of infantile wishes (which as an adult he perceives as a loss of childhood and youth) by substituting gratifications which are now appropriate. Thus he will be able to enjoy adult pleasures.

> *2. Strength of Character.* If the positive aspects of his early infantile experiences with his mother are predominant over their negative aspects, the individual incorporates those experiences into his personality. His ego thus can similarly develop by using positive characteristics of others, thereby gaining character strength (in this description of Klein's ideas, and in our own, the terms his and hers are interchangeable, unless specially defined in relation to sex).

> *3. Ability to adapt to conflicting emotions.* Only "weak" persons avoid inner or outer conflicts, in this formula. "Normal mental

health is based on an interplay in which the capacity for love is predominant."

4. *A balance between the internal psychic life and an adaptation to objective reality.* This balance depends upon some insight into the variety of our contradictory impulses and feelings and the capacity to come to terms with these inner conflicts. An aspect of balance is the adaptation to the external world — an adaptation which does not interfere with the freedom of our own emotions and thoughts. This implies an interaction: An individual's inner life always influences his attitudes towards external reality at the same time that the world of reality tends to adapt his inner life.

5. *An integration of the concept of one's self.* In agreement with almost all practitioners of the psychological sciences, Klein states that there are inner psychic drives which energize our feelings and behaviors. And in keeping with many psychoanalysts, she states that there is an additional inner agency which tends to integrate these drives. She states that this inner agency is love, so that love is both the stimulus and the binding force which integrates the other agencies. Thus the better integrated the man, who can adapt and who can love, "the stronger will be his character, and the greater will be his mental balance."

GROWTH

Adaptation requires that growth take place, and this phenomenon of growth is also emphasized in some psychiatric definitions of normalcy. Thus, Grinker (35) underlines this feature when he describes a significant aspect of normalcy as a "goal changing growth process." We have already seen some of these specific goals in Erikson's description of the eight phases through which the normal man continues to grow as he moves toward new goals.

Perhaps a word may be inserted on the goals of evolution, which stimulated our description of adaptation in the first place. A pithy undergraduate recently summarized evolution as having six phases: 1. To grow larger and more specialized. 2. To emerge from the sea onto the land. 3. To climb up into the trees. 4. To climb down again, and to manufacture tools. 5. To convert tools into weapons. 6. To convert weapons into tools again.

FLEXIBILITY

To return to our thesis, the process of adaptational growth, with its requirement to be able to change its goals, perforce demands another factor. This factor is flexibility. Kubie, in a definitive paper for advanced students on the "Fundamental Nature of the Distinction between Normality and Neurosis" (55) develops this point after showing the lack of flexibility in neurosis. Neurosis, he states, engenders repitition which is automatic and obligatory, being driven by Unconscious urges, and resulting in no improvement in adaptation. Then he writes that the trait by which we clinically distinguish between normality and neurosis centers around the freedom and flexibility to learn through experience, to change, and to adapt to changing external circumstances. "Thus the essence of normality is flexibility, in contrast to the freezing of behavior into patterns of unalterability that characterize every manifestation of the neurotic process, whether in impulses, purposes, acts, thoughts or feelings."

HAPPINESS

In addition to adaptation requiring the features of growth and flexibility, there is yet another component. This component is happiness, as it is described by Ernest Jones. Lest we fall into the trap of moralizing on the subject of happiness and thereby unblushingly subscribe to the hopeful hedonism of those who say that normality *is* happiness, we shall define what Ernest Jones meant by this term.

> Were it necessary to defend Jones against the charge of moralizing, however, I should be happy to do so. Jones was a superb scholar of Freudian psychology, and gifted with a grand intellectual style. In addition to his many contributions on psychoanalytic theory and technique, and his definitive biography of Freud, Jones was responsible for pieces of rather dry wit, and also wrote a short book on figure skating, as well as a quite delightful article on How To Tell Your Friends From Geniuses.

Jones defined happiness in its biopsychological context. Just as lower animals groom themselves when they are apparently satiated, and our children spontaneously may sing when they are contented, happiness to Jones (46) is composed of the capacity for enjoyment, and its expression as self content. The healthy mind, in his view, features both happiness and also efficiency in mental functioning, which in turn is composed of adaptation to reality and a positive social relationship with one's fellow men.

CONSCIOUS CONTROL

So far, we have shown how the psychoadaptational definition of normalcy requires both flexibility and growth as an ongoing process throughout life, with a resultant relationship with others that yields such highly valued qualities as warmth, love and happiness. There remains to be described one more major psychologic and adaptational component of normalcy. This component is the adaptive control, in consciousness, of the impulses and strivings, which are unconscious. In psychodynamic terms, this is expressed by saying that in the normal man, the Ego (which is that structure of the personality that deals with reality and is largely conscious), is in functioning control of the Id (which is the repository of the urges and drives, and is largely unconscious). How is this true?

Again, Kubie develops the concept, this time using a bit of adversary technique. He first shows that in neurosis, there is the predominance of unconscious processes, harking back to the automatic and obligatory behavior in neurosis. He then concludes that "everything [that is] characteristic of the neurotic process can be deduced as a consequence of the domination of behavior by unconscious processes" (55). The repetition of this automatic and obligatory neurotic behavior, which is dominated by the unconscious, fails to produce any insight into the motive for the repetition, nor does it promote adaptation to this motive.

On the other hand, in a state of normalcy, the conscious ego is more frequently able to recognize when unconscious forces are at work, and then effectively to deal with them. The normal man, he states, demonstrates a growing ability to know the unconscious motives which energize his feelings, thereby increasing his ability to use these motives in an adaptive fashion. Kubie then concludes that in normalcy, those areas which are dominated by inaccessibly unconscious forces are continually being shrunk, while those areas which are dominated by conscious and preconscious forces (which forces can enter awareness when necessary) are continually growing.

THE PRAGMATIC NORMAL

So far, we have viewed several definitions of normal which differ so markedly from each other that we doubt whether any one definition will suffice. Instead, we propose that the definition of normal be a pragmatic one which is specifically applicable to the complexities of the human individual.

With this guideline before us, we propose that the pragmatic normal man, who is the practical normal man, has these characteristics:

A. Physically, he shows no signs of severe disease or impairment, nor does he conceive of himself as severely impaired.
B. Psychologically
   1. He neither merits the diagnosis of severe impairment by a diagnosable mental disorder, nor does he conceive of himself as being so impaired.
   2. He shows a trend in the direction of adaptive psychologic growth.
   3. He can Work — independently, exercising at least some initiative.
   4. He can Love — others and in a self enlightened way, love himself. Sexually, he functions enjoyably and adequately.
   5. He can Understand — or have insight into some of his unconscious motives and those of other people.
   6. He can Control — consciously, some of his feelings and behavior, in a manner which is adaptational in reality.
   7. Success — he will have experienced at least some successes.
C. Socially — He will have developed a system of social values which includes:
   1. A sense of justice (which is described in Chapter 7) and therefore a functioning conscience.
   2. Acceptability by some persons who are significant to him; and some acceptability to society as a whole.

Now, in the next chapter, let us examine the concept of disease.

SUMMARY

We have discussed five different definitions of "normal" — the moral normal, the modal normal, the healthy normal, the psycho-adaptational normal, and a pragmatic or practical normal.

The definition of the Moral Normal suffers from subjectivity and inflexibility, and all too frequently eliminates objective data on the very item which is being scrutinized, often because of a psychological defense reaction against being objective. The definition of the Modal Normal, by which the mode or that statistical measurement which occurs most often in a series, is considered to be normal, also suffers when we approach the complexity of the human organism, for a modal man is only theoretically capable of being discovered. So, too, does our definition of the Healthy Normal, which states that the healthy is the normal, for a review of the prevalence of major and minor patterns of disease and disability shows that the man who is healthy in mind and body is a relatively infrequent find. Then we come to the Psychoadaptational Normal, in which we decide that the normal man is one who will continue to grow throughout life, with flexibility that enables him to be able to adapt, both to his own internal or unconscious strivings, and to the external world, resulting in greater efficiency and self satisfaction. Finally we propose in detail a Pragmatic Normal, which is composed of parts of the previous definitions, but which dynamically interrelates them on the biologic, psychologic and sociologic levels.

The Pragmatic Normal man is physically free of severe impairment, is psychologically able to test external reality and use his evaluation of reality to adapt, and is one who sociologically shows a sense of justice.

CHAPTER 6

DISEASE

Having described the nature of positive health and of normalcy in the last chapter, we will now discuss disease, again by using the method of the legislator and the lawyer to show what disease cannot be, before we show precisely what it is. In the prescientific times of history, disease was often a malevolent mystery, frequently in the form of dreaded pestilence. In the Book of Psalms, where man sings of his God which is his fortress, and prays that His truth shall be his sword and his buckler, it is proclaimed that he

> shalt not be afraid for the terror by night;
> nor for the arrow that flieth by day;
> nor for the pestilence that walketh in darkness;
> nor for the destruction that wasteth at noon. (Psalm 91)

But one hundred years ago, a great philosopher-scientist of medicine, Hughlings Jackson, wrote that "Disease is an experiment which is performed by Nature." In the discussion which follows, we shall elaborate various modern definitions of disease that include not only our subjective sense of malevolence and pestilence, but also others which rely upon the objectivity and insights of scientific medicine and psychiatry. We shall begin with the exposure of several popular myths that affect our concept of disease. Then we shall document a definition of disease which is functional both medically and legally. Finally, we shall give a clinical rendering and a surgical dissection of the following terms as they have been defined by the courts: *Sickness, Status, Condition* and *Compulsion.*

MYTHS OF DISEASE

The Myth of Demonic Illness

At a time when experts firmly believed that disease was spawned by the spontaneous generation of invisible agents, and when the infections which followed wounds of war were equally well known to be due to the use of poisoned bullets by the enemy, our concept of the causation of disease was based on a system of demonology. In this system, just as in our modern system of scientific determinism, a cause always proceeds to an effect. But in the demonological system, the evil effects of disease were felt to be the product of a malevolent force or an evil spirit, which often was personified as a demon.

So firmly rooted in our thinking on the cause of disease has the theory of demonic possession become, that a series of brilliant discoveries of disease mechanisms has been misinterpreted to take on the complexion of prescientific illogic, or of emotional reasoning: A major discovery, which one would expect to demolish the demonic myth, was made less than one hundred years ago. This discovery was the proof by Robert Koch, an illustrious professor of medicine at the University of Berlin, that specific bacteria were essential to produce certain specific diseases. Koch showed, using laboratory animals who were infected with anthrax, that a series of four events took place in the linkage between the anthrax bacteria and the disease anthrax.

These four events, which are now known as Koch's postulates in honor of their propositor, have become fixed in the minds of medical men, and are the basis of much misguided thinking concerning disease. Koch showed, as an illustration of his first postulate, that in cases of anthrax, the bacteria of anthrax could be recovered from every case. Secondly, in his laboratory, by using the techniques which were the best of that time, he showed that no other bacteria could be recovered and grown in great numbers. Thirdly, after injecting experimental animals with a large number of these bacteria, these animals became ill with anthrax. And his fourth postulate was a recapitulation of the first three. This recapitulation was illustrated by his showing that from every case of anthrax which had followed his use of the first three postulates, he was able to repeat the process in another experimental animal. Thus finding the bacteria, reproducing them in pure culture, and inoculating an additional animal who was not infected, he showed that this animal had indeed become infected, in a cyclical chain of events.

Because of the great practical value of this proof to a world that was plagued by epidemics, and because of the appeal of its logic, this proof was accepted without noting an additional major factor in the chain between bacteria and infectious disease. That factor is immunity. But immunity did not go unrecognized, even then.

In Koch's own laboratory, on the day following his announcement of his postulates, Professor Dr. Hugo Pettenkorfer, a medical pathologist, performed a significant rebuttal by means of an experiment that now seems overly daring. Pettenkorfer, who had been exposed to anthrax many times both in the laboratory and in the field, ceremoniously breakfasted before his colleagues by spreading over his liverwurst a paste that was made of anthrax bacteria. Aside from some minor gastrointestinal discomfort, he suffered no adverse effects, and never became ill of anthrax. Thus even contemporaneously with Koch, the factor of immunity as a deterrent to disease, or as a method of preventing disease, was bravely and personally demonstrated (18).

We now know that Koch's postulates operate in individuals who have little or no immunity to the bacterium or virus or another "agent" of the disease. But we also know that an immune reaction by the body can completely prevent the bacteria from multiplying in that body, as took place in the case of Professor Dr. Pettenkorfer with his liverwurst. Such an immunity is widespread throughout the world today.

Among city dwellers in the United States who are over forty, more than half show the effect of immunity to tuberculosis. These immune individuals have lymph glands which are located near the root of the lungs, that show clearly on x-ray (these are called Ghon tubercles after their discoverer), which contain live tubercle bacilli. However, these live bacteria which once invaded the body and circulated through many of its parts, have become encapsulated within a firm covering which remains impervious to the passage of bacteria under the usual conditions of immunity. Only when the immunity of the body breaks down to a major degree, usually in association with a combination of physical and emotional stresses, other infections, and malnutrition, that individual may become ill with tuberculosis.

Finding some evidence of the tubercle bacilli in the body usually does *not* prove that the individual is ill with the disease tuberculosis. At the early stage of invasion by these bacteria, for example, it would be possible to recover the bacilli from the blood or body fluids in a large number of persons who go on to develop a harmless Ghon tubercle. The recovery of the bacteria, or even of a fairly large number of tuberculosis bacteria does not mean therefore that the individual is clinically ill with the disease. Yet much of our thinking, both in medicine and in lay circles, revolves around the concept that whenever this bacterium is found, it is the *cause* of the disease.

This bacillus (or any one invasive bacterium) is not the cause of the disease. It is one factor which is necessary in the production of that disease. A great many persons whose bodies harbor live tubercle bacilli thus do not have tuberculosis, even though the bacillus is a necessary factor in the production of the disease. The other factors include the immunity or the resistance of the host, the virulence of the invader, and many other features that are resident both in the disease organism and the host organism.

This confusion of a *cause* with a *necessary factor* is based on a primitive and prescientific concept of disease. For many centuries before Koch who in 1882 had demonstrated the tubercle bacillus, we had little to no objective knowledge of the factors which are necessary to cause a disease. In the absence of such knowledge, we had early substituted a system of demonology or of witchcraft. Hence the malevolent influence of demons was felt to be responsible for a plague, and the spell of a witch or some other vengeful force was felt to be the "cause" of a pox or of phthisis. A well imprinted relic of this belief is present in our language, in which we say that we "caught" a cold, or blame an illness on something we "must have eaten." And even the medical profession participates in the exorcism of demons in the statement that the doctor treats the infection, instead of treating the infected person.

Now demons are by definition evil or bad, and witches are similarly bad, but on probation for good behavior. With this definition, the deeds of demons are similarly evil, so that disease falls into the category of the darkly deviate, and even the devilish. Thus when our infant science of preventive medicine avails us not against many types of infections, we attempt an exorcism when we say that we are "fighting off a nasty cold." Or if we fancy the enemy to be the demon rum, and further find that we are in a state of rout, we note that we are "under the influence." Ultimately, therefore, if we avoid the ill effects of disease, we shall thereby enjoy good health.

In these modern times, when we consciously shun leveling a moral finger at symptoms of disease, and eschew demonology and witchcraft as a cause of disease symptoms, we nonetheless suffer from moments of regression to prescientific reasoning. These regressions appear in the form of phobias and delusions that have emerged from their place in the unconscious mind. In a phobia there is an organized fear of a specific object or act, which is inconsistent with the present conscious thinking of the individual, but is consistent with his past history, and also is associated with marked anxiety. The feared object of the phobia tends to take on demonic qualities because it embodies the concomitance of mystery and anxiety. A delusion, which is a false belief that is inconsistent with the individual's background and the background of his environment, also can be easily imputed to the supernatural because of its unreal, yet compelling quality.

In modern medicine and psychiatry, the practitioner becomes intimately familiar with many phobias such as the fear of germs or of dirt. Even more frequently encountered is the delusion of a somatic illness that cannot be objectively verified despite many competent medical investigations, as in those cases of hard-core hypochondriasis which are based on a delusion of disease. In those cases, the patient's perception of a malevolent force that arises from within his mind has been projected onto a germ or a disease that is objectively not present in his body. By means of this projection, a person in modern times who unconsciously has developed a delusion of disease, leaps backward over the history of medicine, to enter a prescientific state, which is identical in many of its features to the state of demoniacal possession.

The Myth of Dr. Szasz' "Mental Illness"

Having already scrutinized a demonic myth of mental illness in a general way, let us now turn to a particular, and devilish, myth of mental illness. The principal proponent of this latter myth is a well trained but cuttingly controversial psychiatrist, Dr. Thomas L. Szasz. Dr. Szasz states in essence that mental disease, or "the notion of mental illness has outlived whatever usefuless it might have had, so that it now functions merely as a convenient myth. As such it is the true heir to religious myths in general and to the belief in witchcraft in particular; the role of all these belief systems was to act as *social tranquilizers,* thus encouraging the hope that mastery of certain specific problems may be achieved by means of substitutive (symbolic-magical) operations" (90).

After noting that "living is an arduous process [because of] the stresses and strains inherent in the social intercourse of complex human personalities," he attempts to relate mental illness to his definition of problems in living. He writes:

"For it seems to me that at least in our scientific theories of behavior we have failed to *accept* the simple fact that human relations are inherently fraught with difficulties, and that to make them even relatively harmonious requires much patience and hard work. I submit that the idea of mental illness is now being put to work to obscure certain difficulties which at present may be inherent—not that they need be unmodifiable—in the social intercourse of persons. If this is true, the concept functions as a disguise; for instead of calling attention to conflicting human needs, aspirations and values, the notion of mental illness provides an amoral and impersonal thing (an illness) as an explanation for problems in living."

We get some idea of Dr. Szasz' concept of problems of living by his stating that "psychiatry is that contemporary discipline which is concerned with *problems in living.*" He promptly notes that "By problems in living, then, I refer to that truly explosive chain reaction which began with man's fall from divine grace by partaking of the tree of knowledge." "This chain reaction," he writes, "may be reversed by the acquisition of more understanding, but is worsened by man's taking the view that he does not fashion his life and much of the world about him, but merely lives out his fate in a world created by superior beings." The symbolic tree of knowledge in the Garden of Eden, which was planted there by a Superior Being, nonetheless receives a bit of downgrading when Szasz comments, "it is worth noting that a demonologic conception of problems in living gave rise to therapy along theological lines."

To one who prefers a definition of his terms and who uses the syllogistic method, this significant essay by Szasz on "The Myth of Mental Illness" poses a problem in understanding. It is just as difficult to find out what he means by mental illness or problems in living, as it is to follow his reasoning. After he makes a somewhat jumbled denial, for example, of the observation that physical changes in the body or brain can produce mental symptoms, he goes on:

"MENTAL ILLNESS AS A NAME FOR PROBLEMS IN LIVING

The term mental illness is widely used to describe something which is very different than a disease of the brain. Many people today take it for granted that living is an arduous process. Its hardship for modern man, moreover, derives not so much from a struggle for biological survival as from the stresses and strains inherent in the social intercourse of complex human personalities. In this context, the notion of mental illness is used to identify or describe some feature of an individual's so-called personality. Mental illness—as a deformity of the personality, so to speak—is then regarded as the *cause* of the human disharmony. It is implicit in this view that social intercourse between people is regarded as something *inherently harmonious*, its disturbance being due solely to the presence of mental illness in many people. This is obviously fallacious reasoning, for it makes the abstraction mental illness into a *cause*, even though this abstraction was created in the first place to serve only as a shorthand expression for certain types of human behavior. It now becomes necessary to ask: What kinds of behavior are regarded as indicative of mental illness, and by whom?

"The concept of illness, whether bodily or mental, implies *deviation from some clearly defined norm*. In the case of physical illness, the norm is the structural and functional integrity of the human body. Thus, although the desirability of physical health, as such, is an ethical value, what health *is* can be stated in anatomical and physiological terms. What is norm deviation from which is regarded as mental illness? This question cannot be easily answered. But whatever this norm might be, we can be certain of only one thing: namely, that it is a norm that must be stated in terms of *psycho-*

social, ethical, and *legal* concepts. For example, notions such as excessive repression or acting out an unconscious impulse illustrate the use of psychological concepts for judging (so-called) mental health and illness. The idea that chronic hostility, vengefulness, or divorce are indicative of mental illness would be illustrations of the use of ethical norms (that is, the desirability of love, kindness, and a stable marriage relationship). Finally, the widespread psychiatric opinion that only a mentally ill person would commit homicide illustrates the use of a legal concept as a norm of mental health. The norm from which deviation is measured whenever one speaks of a mental illness is a *psychosocial and ethical one.* Yet, the remedy is sought in terms of *medical* measures which—it is hoped and assumed—are free from wide differences of ethical value. The definition of the disorder and the terms in which its remedy are sought are therefore at serious odds with one another. The practical significance of this covert conflict between the alleged nature of the defect and the remedy can hardly be exaggerated."

While there is manifest value to a periodic review of our basic ideas or to a challenge of our current concepts, it seems that many of Szasz' challenges suffer by not being based on a sound foundation. In connection with his statement which is quoted above, one cannot believe that social intercourse is truly regarded as inherently harmonious. Social harmony is a well established ideal, but in most societies, this idea is a wish but not an achievement. And concerning the suggestion that mental illness is the *sole* cause of social disharmony, we feel that any disorder of social harmoniousness must be based on a number of imbricated factors, which include at least the interrelation between two or more individuals and the nature of the society in which this relation takes place, as well as the individual's mental factors, which may be well, ordered, or disordered.

As for his comment the "widespread psychiatric opinion that only a mentally ill person would commit homicide" this appears strange to those of us who read the testimony of psychiatrists at various trials for homicide. In these trials, the psychiatric witnesses are on two different sides of the question, so that even were Dr. Szasz' statement to be true, these trials would manifestly tend to document at least an equal number of psychiatrists with opinions in the negative. There are a few articulate psychiatrists who have agreed with Dr. Szasz on this question but these individuals constitute the exception to the rule. Most American psychiatrists take the rather clinical position that homicide can be committed with method, by mistake, or from madness.

Perhaps a clue to Szasz' negativism, to his use of allegation as a substitute for fact, and to his subjectivised variety of logic, can be gained from his statement which indicates his feelings about law and authority. He writes "Similarly, if a psychiatrist is engaged by a court to determine the sanity of a criminal, he need not fully share the legal authorities' values and intentions in regard to the criminal and the means available for dealing with him. But the psychiatrist is expressly barred from stating, for example, that it is not the criminal who is 'insane' but the men who wrote the law on the basis of which the very actions that are being judged are regarded as 'criminal.' Such an opinion could be voiced, of course, but not in a courtroom, and not by a psychiatrist who makes it his practice to assist the court in performing its daily work."

In commenting on this forceful feeling by Dr. Szasz, we admit that some lawmakers can be insane, and therefore that their laws, or the law itself, can be insane. However, he fails to prove his point when he relies on suspicious innuendo, instead of proving that legislators and legislation are insane. In an overview, one feels that Szasz' challenge by which he states that the concept of mental illness is a myth, not only suffers severely because of its motivations, but is faulty in its substance.

The Bell-shaped Myth of Disease

In our previous discussion of normalcy, we showed that a series of measurements of a single feature of the members of a population, whether that population be composed of herring, people or sidereal bodies, would almost always follow a fixed pattern. In this pattern, most of the measurements are either the same, or else are very close to the measurement which occurs most frequently. The measurement which appears the most often, is called the *mode*. Also in this pattern, the farther away that we proceed from the mode, the fewer the number of individuals do we find. On a graph, this distribution takes the form of an old fashioned dinner bell, or a page-boy hair arrangement, and is called the bell-shaped curve.

We then described the concept which some have put forth, that normalcy consists in being located on the top of the bell, due to possessing a measurement which is equal to the mode (and is called the modal point) or a measurement which is close to the mode, and is therefore within the "shoulders" of the bell-shaped curve. Despite the appeal which this approach makes because of its simplicity, we were forced to reject it.

This rejection was made principally because most members of a human population possess a great many different characteristics. In our human species, when we measure simple features such as a person' height or weight (which in the older tables and in many doctors' offices are made with men's shoes on and women's shoes off) we can draw a bell-shaped curve or a normal curve. But when we take a series of such curves, of which one will show at its modal point a man of average height and weight, another a man who gives no history of heart disease, cancer or stroke in his family or in himself, another one who has the literacy both to read and understand the average application form for a job (an 11th grade achievement), another curve which depicts an individual who has never required admission to a mental hospital and who now shows no signs of mental health impairment, we are vexatiously pressed. When we attempt to fit these different findings together, the curves simply do not fit on top of each other.

We then learned that in any one individual, the more characteristics we measured or graded, the lesser was the likelihood of that individual to possess measurements which resembled those of the greatest number of the population. Thus the more we learn of our complex characteristics, the more deviant we are shown to be. In a study of the physical and mental health of the population, we found that "the modal man is an ideal fiction; ideal, to be sure, but yet a fiction."

But the bell-shaped curve raises its symmetrically formed figure in another area, where it may be applicable to our present problem of defining the nature of disease (91). Certain sociologists have reasoned in a provocative manner on the presence of disease in the community. Their reasoning proceeds in four steps: A certain amount of disease has always been present in the community, along with a much greater amount of health. Since it is always to be found in measurable quantities, disease is part of the nature of the community. The next step in their reasoning can easily be

taken by the agile, and easily missed by the unwary. It is this—
Since disease is a component of the nature of the community,
disease is natural. The final step is at least verbally conclusive—
Since disease is natural, therefore we may not draw a sharp
distinction between disease and other natural states, such as the
state of health.

If we follow this argument, then, disease has always been
present, and presumably will always be with us, so that it exists as
a part of life itself, thus being natural. It is not a very long step
from this point to deny that disease exists as a category, nor is it
too difficult to invoke this variety of reasoning in an attempt to
demonstrate that anything which co-exists with something else
become indistinguishable from that something else. We cannot
agree with this line of thought, because of the violence it wreaks
on the syllogistic process.

A DEFINITION OF DISEASE

Having described some of the myths concerning disease, let us
now give a positive definition of disease. Following this definition
we shall then describe some synonyms of disease and some legal
variations of the meaning of the word disease, particularly attend-
ing to *Sickness, Status, Condition* and *Compulsion.*

A disease is a process which affects an individual's body and
mind, that process being a necessary factor in producing a deformity of structure, impairment of function, or physical or mental
pain, when that deformity, pain or impairment can be objectively
classified by currently acceptable diagnostic standards, and/or
subjectively perceived by the individual. In physical disease, the
body is more palpably affected, and in mental disease, the mind is
more notably affected.

There are many other terms which describe the same process
which we describe as a disease. Two of these terms which are often
used by practicing physicians are *disorder* and *illness.* In law we
may differentiate disease from disorder or illness, and also special-
ly define the term *sickness,* as will be documented below. In
public health, we also use the term *condition,* which may refer to
a wide range of subjectively perceived or objectively diagnosed

disease phenomena, from influenza through stroke, which are among the ten most common chronic conditions that have been described on page 88.

SICKNESS, STATUS, CONDITION AND COMPULSION

I. Sickness

In constitutional times, our founding fathers established a United States District, or the District of Columbia, as the seat of the federal government. This district, "not exceeding ten miles square," was required to be governed by the Congress, rather than by the nine states whose ratification put the Constitution into effect. Since those times, the Congress has continued to legislate for this small but active district, and the courts of the District of Columbia have been notably responsive to federal legislation. One such act by Congress in 1947 is a benchmark in the delineation of the legislative meaning of the work *sickness,* and possibly more significant, of the interpretation of this word by our courts.

In 1947, when many veterans of World War II had returned home with neuro-psychiatric disabilities, and the awareness of psychiatry by the general public was rapidly proliferating, an Act of Congress entitled "Rehabilitation of Alcoholics" was passed, and embodied in the District of Columbia Code (§ 24-501). The purpose of this act was to:

> "... to establish a program for the rehabilitation of alcoholics, promote temperance, and provide for the medical, psychiatric, and other scientific treatment of chronic alcoholics ..."

Taking appropriate note of the brotherly relation between the Executive, Legislative and Judicial branches of our government, the Congress by this act gave specific instructions to the courts by providing that:

> "the courts of the District of Columbia are hereby authorized to take judicial notice of the fact that a chronic alcoholic is a sick person and in need of proper medical, institutional, advisory, and rehabilitative treatment, and the court is authorized to direct that he receive appropriate medical, psychiatric, or other treatment as provided under the terms of this chapter."

The D.C. Code § 24-501 (1961 ed) then proceeds to define some important features of the term "chronic alcoholic." It must be noted here that in medicine the term "chronic" usually refers to a condition which has been present for three months or longer, such as the chronic conditions, which we have already described on page 87.

In psychiatry, however, an additional (and startling) definition of "chronic" appeared in 1968. In the *Diagnostic and Statistical Manual of Mental Disorders,* published that year, an eminently qualified committee of the American Psychiatric Association gives the following interpretation of the term "chronic." In connection with Organic Brain Disorders (which are disorders of mental function that are associated with, or caused by an impairment of brain tissue function), this *Manual* states (p. 22): "it is important to distinguish acute from chronic brain disorders because of marked differences in the course of illness, prognosis and treatment. The terms indicate primarily whether the brain pathology and its accompanying brain syndrome [the term syndrome is used in medicine to mean a correlated group of signs and symptoms] is reversible. Since the same etiology or cause may produce either temporary or permanent brain damage, a brain disorder which appears reversible (acute) at the beginning may prove later to have left permanent brain damage, and a persistent organic brain syndrome which will then be diagnosed chronic." Thus chronic means irreversible, a term which is incompatible with the therapeutic optimism of most medical and psychiatric practitioners.

The District of Columbia Codes' definition of a "chronic alcoholic," who has already been defined by fiat as a sick person, was then set forth.

A chronic alcoholic is defined in the Act:

"The term 'chronic alcoholic' means any person who chronically and habitually uses alcoholic beverages to the extent that he has lost the power of self-control with respect to the use of such beverages, or while under the influence of alcohol endangers the public morals, health, safety, or welfare."

In the trials and tribulations of a man named Dewitt Easter (Easter v. District of Columbia 1966), these definitions were utilized in a manner which has made legal precedent. In that case, the U.S. Court of Appeals D.C. Circuit (361 F.2d 50, 1966) first observed that the chronic alcoholic is a medically and psychiatrically sick person. Because of this sickness, his "power of self-control" as mentioned above, and we feel his entire mental state, is adversely affected. The court held that a chronic alcoholic does not have the mental state which is necessary for him to be judged criminally responsible for appearing drunk in public.

The court stated "since public intoxication of a chronic alcoholic is not a crime, to convict one of it as though it were, would also constitute cruel and unusual punishment" in violation of the Constitution. The court also noted, with a tone of what appears to be avuncular advice, that commitment for treatment to a psychiatric facility may be ordered by a lower court. The higher court then reversed Easter's conviction for having been "drunk or intoxicated in any street, alley, park or parking. . . ."

Thus a specific sickness, in this case, that of chronic alcoholism, has received a quite specific treatment by the court, defining the term sickness in a manner which differs distinguishably, although to a minor degree, from that which has been used by experts in the fields of legislation and specialties of medicine. Of what value are these definitions? They are of practical value in our system by which we dispense justice, and they become necessary in the area where both medicine and law are simultaneously involved, particularly where the nature and quality of the individual's mental state is at bar.

Yet in this context, "sickness" is essentially the same as a disease or disorder of the entire person. Such a disease or disorder affects his personality and his physical status or condition in such a way that it specifically imposes a chronic disability on him. If the word sickness or status were to have a more exclusively specific meaning, such as one of the 22 different words for snow in the Eskimo language, we could semantically be more precise. Such a specific definition does appear in the specialty of neurology, where "Status epilepticus" describes a rare and occasionally fatal condition in which one seizure proceeds to another, without the usual long interval of freedom from convulsions between seizures. But in the law, as we have seen from the decisions which have been described above, we cannot correctly distinguish a sickness from a disorder, from a disease, or from a disordered or diseased status or condition.

II. Status, or Condition?

A feature of the usage of many drugs is the tendency to repeat the use of the particular drug. This tendency is seen with most drugs which affect an individual's feelings or behavior, so that because of this effect they are called psychoactive drugs. Regardless of whether the use of these psychoactive drugs is associated with signs of withdrawal, the repetition of usage is a characteristic of the problem. From the point of view of the individual's behavior, then, psychoactive drugs may be associated with *behavioral addiction.*

In another form of addiction, a human individual can become habituated or addicted to a drug after he has been given repeated doses of the drug, regardless of his mental state. This assumption is based primarily on a body of experience with lower animals who in the laboratory can be injected regularly, and then later show an apparent desire for the drug (Masserman). These animals demonstrate signs of withdrawal when they are deprived of the drug. Most students on this subject consider this another variety of addiction, and have described it as a *physiological addiction.* However, it is not our purpose here to discuss drug addiction any further, except to introduce the use of the term "status" or "condition" in contrast to "disease" when that status is one of addiction.

A case history which demonstrates many of the sad and sordid features of addiction, will be given here. Because of humanist considerations, identifying data have been altered despite the fact that this history was required to be given in testimony in open court, and hence is in the public domain.

> Thank you for referring John Doe, (date of birth November 24, 1940) currently a patient at Padlock Hospital, Chart No. 01-32-95, for neurological, psychiatric, and psychological consultation.
>
> This thirty-year-old Caucasian male was admitted to the above Hospital under Arizona Revised Statutes 13-1621, following charges of murder, robbery, and assault with a deadly weapon, on November 8, 1969.
>
> My examination, which lasted 2 1/2 hours, followed a study of previous medical material, letters by the patient before November 8, 1969, as well as letters subsequent to that period, letters from the patient's mother, and a telephone interview with her.

The patient states that he left Los Angeles on the night of November 7, driving his car, with an intense fear of people following him, and that he watched as often as he could to see if he were being followed. He also sniffed at least twenty-two tubes of glue while driving all night to Phoenix. The reason that he left Los Angeles was that he had felt rejected by his friend, Bob, with whom he had spent the early part of the night. He has had a relationship with Bob since he was nineteen, and Bob fourteen, in which, "I would really feel good, really feel free, like nothing else ever." Over the years, the patient and Bob would spend time with each other in Los Angeles and sometimes go to Mexico together, and occasionally would go with Tom, another friend. Homosexual experiences were a portion of the picture, but only secondary to his feeling of release. Promiscuity, as the patient put it, was committed only when he was under the influence of glue sniffing.

Recently, Bob has taken up with a girl whose name is Bev, and the three of them would take Acid and go to a drive-in color movie. "It makes a lot more of the movie, but I'd get freaky and get afraid, and I'd try to hide under the floorboards."

In 1965, the patient had suffered a previous rejection by Bob. "He hurt me. Even kindness can hurt me sometimes. Yes, I tried to kill myself, so I used glue. But there was moisture in the glue rag, and I just sat there in my car for five hours and watched my engine burn up. I felt I was a failure at being a failure." The patient recently registered in a hotel under Bob's name.

"Next time I'd go shoot me a cop; that figures."

The patient does not now recall any of the episodes of the alleged shooting with which he is charged. The evidence shows that he held up a drive-in movie, and shot and killed the assistant manager. We know that immediately previous to the killing, he had seen a movie, *Butch Cassidy and the Sundance Kid*, which depicts migratory robbers, shooting, wounding and execution at the end.

The patient was born in 1940 in Mancelona, Michigan, moved to California in 1945, and to Phoenix in 1969. His father is described as a sixty-year-old self-employed house painter who works all day, but also nights and weekends at a church. "I never had anything to do with him—no, I never played games or watched sports with him either."

The mother is described as a fifty-four-year-old woman with a heart condition, whom the patient experienced as having been overprotective all his life. She would say, "Don't do this or you'll get hurt," and "Don't climb a tree before you fall and break your neck." The one altercation he remembers between his parents ended, about 1952, in the father saying, "L. B. Foster can kiss my ass," and stalking out of the house for five hours.

There is a brother two years older and a sister ten years younger, but the patient has very little communication with either, although he thinks that both are well.

The family history includes the mother's sister having been admitted to a state hospital in Tennessee, with a diagnosis of schizophrenia. Both her brothers are alcoholics. One brother, the mother's twin, has a violent temper and is addicted to drinking. The mother's aunt has epilepsy.

The mother describes her having been in "active" labor at the time of his delivery for 3 days, and that he was premature by 2 weeks. He was a colicky infant. At age 1 1/2, "he was grabbed by a colored man at home," and subsequently had nightmares. At age 4 he had pneumonia, after an attack of tonsillitis, and was delirious, screaming frequently. At age 4, he thought he saw a man on a tractor chasing him and continued to see him for four days. He had nightmares and screamed.

He did poorly in school, because he "refused to read, and my mother did not whip me for that." But Mrs. Page, his schoolteacher, "picked on me for anything and whipped me at school." Also, the school bullies beat him up, because (he thought) he was fat.

When he was twelve, an adult neighbor began taking him and another youngster into a garage to perform fellatio on the two boys. When this adult's mother died, his sister and brother-in-law "put him in the State Hospital." He (the patient) completed the tenth grade of school, but during his fifteenth year of age he was expelled from three schools.

At about 13, he had an undescended testicle, for which he received hormone treatment. Later, he lost 60 pounds in order to join the Marine Corps. He was in the Marine Corps in 1958 for about four months, but was discharged under conditions of unsuitability. In 1960, a psychiatric social worker's interview noted the presence of depression.

He has had a spotty work history, despite some ability at house painting and draftsmanship.

He has begun to use numerous drugs heavily since at least 1960 and has used methedrine (speed), mescaline, glue (toluene), and at least 200 trips with LSD, as well as heavy use of alcohol and marijuana. Concerning his obtaining LSD without money, he said, "I know people who deal with them" (them refers to people who intend to do him harm). "They give it to you in a drink. Once I woke up in Yuma." (Why?) "Well, it's the thing to do." (What good does it do them to do it to you?) "Sometimes I don't know which end is up. I don't like it."

In 1969, he was admitted to the Habor General Hospital in Los Angeles, where he stated that he had an argument with the doctor.

"I had paralysis, and I had to lean on him to stand up and hit him." The patient laughed with full inspiratory pauses after each laugh, but with a remote look in his eyes, as he describes this.

In August, 1968, he was admitted to the hospital for infectious hepatitis following the use of a contaminated needle for drug injection, with a history of another individual having been infected at the same drug session by the same needle. A diagnosis was made of antisocial personality. In September 1968, he was readmitted with weakness and sensory loss in the extremities, spreading upwards to his face, and affecting his speech briefly, with a high protein content and no cells in the spinal fluid. Electromyogram showed a denervation pattern in the extremities, more prominently in the lower extremities. A diagnosis of Guillain-Barre syndrome, or myelo-radiculo-neuropathy, was made.

In December 1968, while driving his automobile, "it went out of control" shearing off a power pole, striking a garage in an apartment building, demolishing two cars in this garage, in which the water pipes were burst by the impact, flooding the building. He was thrown 40 feet from the car and became unconscious. He was not booked for drunk driving.

On admission there was a fracture of the skull in the vicinity of the right orbit, and multiple abrasions. There was a fracture of the right scapula and a perforating fracture of the right seventh rib and a hemothorax, as well as bilateral pneumonia. He improved medically. Psychiatric consultation noted depression, and he signed out against advice.

In September 1969, he complained of "people watching, bugging and supervising him." A psychiatrist made the diagnosis of paranoia.

He thinks that he began to hallucinate frightening things when he was not taking drugs, since 1963. The hallucinations are sometimes human in form, except that they are 30 to 40 feet tall. Sometimes he would see people staring through a hedge at him when they weren't there, and he would sometimes see nonexistent guns trained on him from within the ivy. "Once, in early 1969, I went out in the daytime and cut the ivy back, because people might be there." He does not go out during the day because "people watch me, and they can't see me as well at night."

No information could be obtained on a heterosexual sex life.

The patient has frequent blackouts but does not know whether these are due to other people giving him drugs of which he is unaware.

GENERAL PHYSICAL EXAMINATION: Shows a man looking slightly older than his stated age, with some graying hair, weak musculature, a protuberant abdomen, a small penis and testicles, and soft buttocks.

The right palpebral fissure is smaller than the left, and there is a latent external squint, giving his facial expressions a bizarre appearance.

There are rounded depigmentations in both antecubital spaces which resemble cigarette burns that were superimposed on needle puncture marks. The right arm shows a tatoo of a skeleton who is riding a motor scooter.

There are scars over the left eyebrow, the left mastoid bone, and left frontal bone, and a drainage scar below the right fifth rib.

Except for an impure second heart sound over the apex, examination of the thoracic and abdominal viscera was negative.

NEUROLOGICAL EXAMINATION: Uncovered in the left retina an unusually large inferior vein, and in the left ear there is a scar in the lower half of the eardrum.

There is an area of diminished sensitivity to light touch and to pinprick over the left forearm on the radial side, which extends to the dorsal portion of the fingers, in the distribution of the lateral antebrachial cutaneous nerve. Vibratory perception to a 128 d.v. tuning fork was diminished over both feet. Cranial nerves, motor and sensory status were otherwise within normal limits, noting that the patient was very "ticklish" and muscularly weak.

SPECIAL EXAMINATION: Patient is right-eyed, righthanded, and clumsy with both feet. His perception of pitch is adequate, and he sings accurately.

PSYCHOLOGICAL EXAMINATION: Shows no gross organic mental syndrome. He is able to subtract serial sevens from 102 accurately and rapidly. He retains 8 digits forward and 7 digits backwards. His stream of talk is frequently delivered in a low and slow tone, but at times is characterized by loud chuckling and frank laughter. When I asked about his letter in which he disinherited his father, he chuckled and said, "Of what?" Starting to laugh, with his body almost immobile, he said, "If I get out of here, I'd starve to death, unless I asked my dad for money. That's funny." He then laughed for approximately eight seconds and stopped suddenly, with his eyebrows knitted and the corners of his mouth turned down.

He said he never had any happy times in his life, except for a few hours, and these were with Bob. He could never control his impulses, he states, and he has never had any heroes. He continued that, "people are no good. They are a bunch of rats; it's not wise to trust anyone."

In response to the question, "What is a conscience?," he said, "I used to have one ... maybe around 1960 ... I used to feel guilty, and I had complexes, but then I found out what people are really like now."

(What do right-thinking people do with their lives?) "I don't know

any people like that." (But what would they possibly do?) "How
can you expect me to know, when I don't know any?"

(What do you expect to happen to you?) "I'll get killed some way
or the other." (How do you feel you will take that?) "It beats the
hell out of life."

Drawings of a house, tree and persons show an empty house with
a threatening front. The tree is typical of that seen in depressive and
suicidal individuals. The person of the same sex is small, pejorative
and a cartoon. The person of the opposite sex is full size, nude and
without hands or feet, but she shows the black and closed eyes
which are drawn by paranoid persons, as well as severe shading, the
latter being seen in anxiety.

DIAGNOSTIC IMPRESSION:
  1. Paranoid state with psychosis, with delusions of persecution and
depression.
  2. Drug dependence on toluene, alcohol, methedrine, and the hallu-
cinogens mescaline and LSD, with presumptive damage to liver, brain
and bone marrow.

DISCUSSION:
  The presence of depression with marked anxiety, and of hallucinations that are not temporally associated with drugs, rule out a diagnosis of antisocial personality disorder or other psychopathic disorders as
the principal diagnosis at this time.

PROGNOSIS:
  Prognosis is grave. Unless the patient can appropriately contemplate
the possibility that his fears and doubts are his own and are not
exclusively produced by other people, and by authority figures in his
personal community, he cannot improve his psychological status. If he
were permitted to continue his present use of drugs, he will live less
than five years more.

RECOMMENDATIONS FOR TREATMENT:
  That he be given inpatient psychiatric care in a maximum security
environment until he should be able radically to alter his feelings and
behavior in the direction of the acceptable norm.

  In keeping with the Arizona law at that time, he had been found
guilty on all charges by the jury, and was now before the same jury in
a second trial. This trial's purpose was to determine whether he was
sane or insane, under the McNaghten rules, of which a significant
feature is the understanding of right and wrong.

  The patient's ability to reason and to understand was reviewed by
additional questions. A question from the Wechsler intelligence test
was used — "In what ways are an orange and a banana alike?" The

patient said, "they are not related." I asked "How?" and he said
"They are different type things."

Q. Would anyone think that they are related?

A. They are food . . . just so you can eat them both, but one's
mushy and the other is in segments, and bananas give me heart-
burn.

Q. What is the difference between right and wrong?

A. I didn't think I was anymore wrong than they.

Q. Who are they?

A. The police.

Q. How are the police wrong?

A. They lie a lot, they do that way all the time.

Q. How do you feel when somebody else does something wrong?

A. I wouldn't pay that much attention to it . . . I was robbed
once — I was working in a gas station.

Q. Were you shaken up by the robbery?

A. I figured I would help you get the money if you want it that bad.
It don't mean that much to me.

Q. When you see other people doing things that are a lot like things
that you do, how do you feel?

A. Nothing, I watch too many movies.

Q. What feelings do you have about people punishing a child?

A. Ha ha ha — I don't know. As a child I wondered why I was
punished.

Q. If you were punished differently would it have made a difference
in your life?

A. Punishment would have made me more rebellious.

Q. What feelings do people have when they fall in love?

A. It has been so long I can't remember . . . I got burned. Sue — I
was 20. She started using me as a taxicab.

Q. How do people show that they are happy?

A. You mean when I'm happy; I sit there and be gloomy and can be
happy. You know what funny is and not happy? I can be
laughing my head off and be sad, sad, sad.

Q. How long have you wanted to die?

A. Since about 1963.

Q. Do you have more hallucinations when you are depressed?

A. Yes, I never thought of that.

Q. Have you ever attacked a hallucination with a gun?

A. Yeah, a couple of years ago. I had a pistol with me. I was freaked
out and I would have shot but I had someone with me.

Q. Have you ever planned to attack a hallucination?

A. Usually I don't unless they are coming at me then I do.

Q. Your relation with the law has been a criminal one. Is there
anything wrong in that relationship?

A. No. They arrested me for something I didn't do. If they arrest me for something I did do then I do time.

Q. How about taking a life?

A. I've been burned before. You gotta die sometime. If I go around worrying about someone else's troubles I will be in sad shape.

At the conclusion of this "insanity" trial, the jury reached a verdict while its female members were weeping. They found the accused to be sane, under the McNaghten rules that were imposed, but they did not recommend a sentence of death. Instead, they recommended life imprisonment.

III. Status

The story of this patient whom we have just described, his case history, (or the testimony before the court, depending on one's orientation at the moment) was given in Arizona, where antisocial personality disorders, the psychopathic personality or psychopathic state are not legally defined as a "disease" at this time. Also in Arizona, it is not currently a crime to be addicted to the use of narcotics.

Yet just across the Colorado River, a California statute made it a criminal offense for a person either to use narcotics or to be addicted to the use of narcotics. In a major case before the Supreme Court of the United States (Robinson v. California 370 U.S. 660, 1962), this statute was held to be unconstitutional because of its being cruel and unusual punishment, which is generally prohibited by the VIII Amendment.

In Robinson v. California, a man was convicted under this statute, after a jury trial had heard very specific evidence. One Robinson showed marks which precisely resembled needle tracks, in the vicinity of the veins of both arms, signs of infection following injection into these areas, and admitted to having used narcotics in the past. The California trial judge had instructed the jury that the statute made it a misdemeanor:

"... for a person 'either to use narcotics, or to be addicted to the use of narcotics. . . .' That portion of the statute referring to the use of narcotics is based upon the 'act' of using. That portion of the statutes referring to 'addicted to the use' or narcotics is said to be a status or condition and not an act. It is a continuing offense and differs from most other offenses in the fact that [it] is chronic rather than acute; that it continues after it is complete and subjects the offender to arrest at any time before he reforms. The existence of such a chronic condition may be ascertained from a single examination, if the characteristic reactions of that condition be found present."

In reversing this conviction, the Supreme Court held that the addiction was a disease rather than an offense, and that this disease merited medical consideration, rather than punishment. Mr. Justice Stewart wrote, in the majority opinion:

"It is unlikely that any State at this moment in history would attempt to make it a criminal offense for a person to be mentally ill, or a leper, or to be afflicted with a venereal disease. A State might determine that the general health and welfare require that the victims of these and other human afflictions be dealt with by compulsory treatment, involving quarantine, confinement, or seque-stration. But, in the light of contemporary human knowledge, a law which made a criminal offense of such a disease would doubtless be universally thought to be an infliction of cruel and unusual punishment in violation of the Eighth and Fourteenth Amendments. See *Francis v. Resweber*, 329 U.S. 459."

"We cannot but consider the statute before us as of the same category. In this Court, counsel for the State recognized that narcot-ic addiction is an illness. Indeed, it is apparently an illness which may be contracted innocently or involuntarily. We hold that a state law which imprisons a person thus afflicted as a criminal, even though he was never touched any narcotic drug within the State or been guilty of any irregular behavior there, inflicts a cruel and unusual punishment in violation of the Fourteenth Amendment. To be sure, imprisonment for ninety days is not, in the abstract, a punishment which is either cruel or unusual. But the question cannot be considered in the abstract. Even one day in prison would be a cruel and unusual punishment for the 'crime' of 'having a common cold.' The Justice continued, with equal force and clarity:

"We are not unmindful that the vicious evils of the narcotics traffic have occasioned the grave concern of government. There are, as we have said, countless fronts on which those evils may be legitimately attacked. We deal in this case only with an individual provision of a particularized local law as it has so far been inter-preted by the California courts.

Reversed."

Thus we see how a status or condition in the particular case of addiction to drugs has been redefined to mean disease. In a separate but concurring opinion, Mr. Justice Douglas noted the specific section of the Welfare and Institutions Code of California (§ 5350) which provides for civil commitment of habitual addicts, in a reference to the concept of confinement for the purpose of treatment, rather than for the purpose of punishment. He points out:

> "Cruel and unusual punishment results not from confinement, but from convicting the addict of a crime. The purpose of § 11721 is not to cure, but to penalize. Were the purpose to cure, there would be no need for a mandatory jail term of not less than ninety days. . . . A prosecution for addiction, with its resulting stigma and irreparable damage to the good name of the accused, cannot be justified as a means of protecting society, where a civil commitment would do as well. Indeed, in § 5350 of the Welfare and Institutions Code, California has expressly provided for civil proceedings for the commitment of habitual addicts. Section 11721 is, in reality, a direct attempt to punish those the State cannot commit civilly. This prosecution has no relationship to the curing of an illness. Indeed, it cannot, for the prosecution is aimed at penalizing an illness, rather than at providing medical care for it. We would forget the teachings of the Eighth Amendment if we allowed sickness to be made a crime and permitted sick people to be punished for being sick. This age of enlightenment cannot tolerate such barbarous action."

IV. Compulsion: Does the Compulsion Fit the Crime? *Powell v. Texas*

In Austin, Texas, one Leroy Powell, a 66-year-old man whose principal occupation was that of shoe shine boy at a local tavern, was well known as a revolving door alcoholic. Since 1949, he had been convicted of being intoxicated in public approximately one hundred times. With each conviction, he was fined $25 in Bastrop County, Texas, but only $20 in adjacent Travis County, yet was unable to pay the fine, for the simple reason that he routinely spent his earnings on wine, which he had promptly consumed. He would then be sent to jail where he attempted to work off the fines at a rate of $5 a day in confinement. Because of his trips in and out of jail being so frequent, and of their being performed with the graceless lack of control that is shown by a man who is trapped in a revolving door, he was called a "revolving door drunk."

In December, 1966, Powell was once more tried in the court of Travis County for public intoxication, under a Texas statute which provides "whoever shall get drunk or be found in a state of intoxication in any public place . . . shall be fined not exceeding one hundred dollars." The arresting officer testified on the physical facts, as had many before him, that Powell had been discovered on an Austin street while staggering about and smelling of alcohol. But at this trial, a new approach was struck, which ultimately was ruled upon in a 5 to 4 decision by the Supreme Court of the United States.

The Counsel who defended Powell pleaded that he suffered from a compulsion to drink, which was a symptom of the disease of chronic alcoholism, and that this disease was a defense against the charge. This defense was based on the comment of a prominent Texas psychiatrist, who was a former president of the Texas Medical Association. Davis Wade, M.D., defined a chronic alcoholic as an involuntary drinker who is powerless not to drink and who loses his self control over his drinking. When Powell was sober, he stated, he knew the difference between right and wrong, and his taking the first drink was done by a voluntary exercise of his will. (Our medical colleague had manifestly sophisticated himself with several aspects of the law. The psychiatrist was referring to the rule in the law which is called the irresistible impulse rule, and also called the "loss of control" rule. This rule excuses from criminal liability those persons who, due to a mental disease, have lost "freedom of will," or the "power . . . to choose between the right and wrong," or the capacity "to refrain from doing wrong") (49).

But the exercise of his will, he went on, was under the exceedingly strong influence of a compulsion. As to the quantitative strength of this compulsion, Dr. Wade said, "these individuals have a compulsion, and this compulsion, while not completely overpowering, is a very strong influence, an exceedingly strong influence, as this compulsion coupled with the firm belief in their minds that they are going to be able to handle it, causes their judgment to be somewhat clouded."

Powell himself testified that, as a rule, he could not control his drinking. But he admitted that on the morning of the trial, he had taken a single drink and no more. It was learned that Powell had no money with which to buy the drink, but that it had been given to him, free. The question was thus raised as to whether Powell's particular revolving door had been controlled, and therefore was a controllable one.

Nevertheless, Powell's attorney argued that he was a chronic alcoholic who was compelled to become intoxicated, and once he became intoxicated, he could not avoid appearing in public in an intoxicated condition. Thus Powell's acts, he pleaded were not of his own volition, and therefore he may not be punished for them. But the County Court rejected this argument, found Powell guilty and again imposed a fine for $20. However, the Texas court entered in its judgement the following material as "findings of fact" that were submitted by defense counsel:

(1) That chronic alcoholism is a disease which destroys the afflicted person's will power to resist the constant, excessive consumption of alcohol.

(2) That a chronic alcoholic does not appear in public by his own volition but under a compulsion symptomatic of the disease of chronic alcoholism.

(3) That Leroy Powell, defendant herein, is a chronic alcoholic who is afflicted with the disease of chronic alcoholism.

Since Powell could not appeal his case in the Texas court system, he appealed directly to the U.S. Supreme Court, saying that punishing him for public intoxication under this particular condition was a cruel and unusual punishment that was prohibited by the VIII Amendment.

The Supreme Court was urged to strike down his conviction by briefs filed on behalf of the American Civil Liberties Union, the American Medical Association, the North American Judges Association, the National Council on Alcoholism, and numerous other organizations concerned with the plight of the alcoholic. The Supreme Court affirmed his conviction by a 5 to 4 vote. But the five justices who comprised the majority could not agree on a single opinion and filed three opinions; the four dissenting justices filed a single dissenting opinion.

Leroy Powell's treatment by the highest court in the land demonstrates the difficulty of merging the disciplines of law and psychology in the task of defining criminal liability. Convinced that the threat of criminal liability can deter, but bothered by the stigma of moral culpability that accompanies criminal conviction, the law requires that for constitutional exculpation, an accused must demonstrate not only the influence of psychological pressures upon him but also the fact that these pressures deprived him of every last shred of freedom of conscious choice.

Is There a Clear and Present Compulsion?

Unlike its definition in general usage, in which the word compulsion means a compelling restraint, an obligation or a coercion, the word compulsion has a specialized meaning in psychology. To the psychologist or psychiatrist, a compulsion is a symptom which often is found in a person with an Obsessive-Compulsive Disorder or Obsessive-Compulsive Trait. A compulsion is a regressive emotional striving, which repetitively impels an individual to perform psychologically significant acts which seem unreasonable both to him and to most objective observers, when this striving causes him to perform these acts despite an attempt consciously to control them, and to suffer anxiety as a consequence.

A mild variety of compulsion is seen in normal children and adults, who keep a continual tally of objects, demonstrating a counting compulsion. For an aircraft controller, an accountant or surgeon to be occupied with the precise count of airplanes, sums or sponges is considered a useful phenomenon, and may, in fact, enhance his normalcy in functioning. Similarly a cleanliness compulsion, when it is very mild in its manifestations and when it is performed in a setting that tolerates such behavior, also can be within normal limits. But psychiatrists are familiar with patients who have a cleanliness compulsion who wash their hands so often and scrub them so clean, that their skin becomes inflamed and may itself require treatment. In another pathological form, the cleanliness compulsion, or ablutomania, produces a secondary pathological result.

> A young woman was referred by a male former patient, who had attempted to be friendly with her. She complained of having become unable to have sexual intercourse.
> In preparation, she would have bathed with extreme care. But after being undressed, when a man would attempt to embrace her, she would then retreat to the bathroom. There she would gargle with a gentle germicide, again cleanse her axillae and other creases of the

body and the anus, and then take a very long douche. After many minutes of this activity, making occasional attempts at conversation with the water running, from behind the locked bathroom door, she would feel fairly well prepared. On emerging, however, she observed that "men somehow seem to lose their ardor for me."

Another common compulsion which appears as a mild manifestation in normal individuals, but which in a severe form can be a disruptive symptom of an obsessive compulsive disorder, is a touching compulsion. Thus we rub our fingers over the smooth surface of a table, or the texture of a utensil, just as we rub the patina of a bronze sculpture. We test the feeling of sturdiness of a new chair, the satisfying feel and thunking sound as we slam shut the door of a new automobile. We clap an average size man on the shoulder, or a professional football player on his hip guard. A normal child may carry about his security blanket with him, gaining from its touch one additional bit of mothering, or of Mother.

But for a description of a pathological touching compulsion, we are indebted to John C. Nemiah, M.D. (69) who reproduces a tale told by a layman, which comprises a brilliant diagnostic document.

"Amid darkness and gloom, occasionally broken by flashes of lightning, the stranger related to me, as we sat at the table in the library, his truly touching history. . . .

"There was one thing that I loved better than the choicest gift which could be bestowed upon me, better than life itself — my mother; at length she became unwell, and the thought that I might possibly lose her now rushed into my mind for the first time; it was terrible, and caused me unspeakable misery, I may say horror. My mother became worse, and I was not allowed to enter her apartment, lest by my frantic exclamations of grief I might aggravate her disorder. I rested neither day nor night, but roamed about the house like one distracted. Suddenly I found myself doing that which even at the time struck me as being highly singular; I found myself touching particular objects that were near me, and to which my fingers seemed to be attracted by an irresistible impulse. It was now the table or the chair that I was compelled to touch; now the bellrope; now the handle of the door; now I would touch the wall, and the next moment stooping down, I would place the point of my finger upon the floor: and so I continued to do day after day; frequently I would struggle to resist the impulse, but invariably in vain. I have even rushed away from the object, but I was sure to return, the impulse was too strong to be resisted: I quickly hurried back, compelled by the feeling within me to touch the object. Now, I need not tell you that what impelled me to these actions was the desire to prevent my mother's death; whenever I touched any particular object, it was with the view of baffling the evil chance, as you would call it — in this instance my mother's death.

"A favourable crisis appeared in my mother's complaint, and she recovered; this crisis took place about six o'clock in the morning; almost simultaneously with it there happened to myself a rather remarkable circumstance connected with the nervous feeling which was rioting in my system. I was lying in bed in a kind of uneasy doze, the only kind of rest which my anxiety, on account of my mother, permitted me at this time to take, when all at once I sprang up as if electrified, the mysterious impulse was upon me, and it urged me to go without delay, and climb a stately elm behind the house, and touch the topmost branch; otherwise — you know the rest — the evil chance would prevail. Accustomed for some time as I had been, under this impulse, to perform extravagant actions, I confess to you that the difficulty and peril of such a feat startled me; I reasoned against the feeling and strove more strenuously than I had ever done before; I even made a solemn vow not to give way to temptation, but I believe that nothing less than chains, and those strong ones, could have restrained me. The demoniac influence, for I can call it nothing else, at length prevailed; it compelled me to rise, to dress myself, to descend the stairs, to unbolt the door, and to go forth; it drove me to the foot of the tree, and it compelled me to climb the trunk; this was a tremendous task, and I only accomplished it after repeated falls and trials. When I had got amongst the branches, I rested for a time, and then set about accomplishing the remainder of the ascent; this for some time was not so difficult, for I was now amongst the branches; as I approached the top, however, the difficulty became greater, and likewise the danger; but I was a light boy, and almost as nimble as a squirrel, and, moreover, the nervous feeling was within me, impelling me upward. It was only by means of a spring, however, that I was enabled to touch the top of the tree; I sprang, touched the top of the tree, and fell a distance of at least twenty feet, amongst the branches; had I fallen to the bottom I must have been killed, but I fell into the middle of the tree, and presently found myself astride upon one of the boughs; scratched and bruised all over, I reached the ground, and regained my chamber unobserved; I flung myself on my bed quite exhausted; presently they came to tell me that my mother was better — they found me in the state which I have described, and in a fever besides. The favourable crisis must have occurred just about the time that I performed the magic touch; it certainly was a curious coincidence, yet I was not weak enough, even though a child, to suppose that I had baffled the evil chance by my daring feat.

"Indeed, all the time that I was performing these strange feats, I knew them to be highly absurd, yet the impulse to perform them was irresistible — a mysterious dread hanging over me till I had given way to it; even at that early period I frequently used to reason within myself as to what could be the cause of my propensity to touch, but of course I could come to no satisfactory conclusion respecting it; being heartily ashamed of the practice, I never spoke of it to any one should observe my weakness."

In modern practice, the psychotherapist works with persons who have compulsive problems (as opposed to an occasional compulsive act in a normal person) when these problems are a feature of an Obsessive-Compulsive Disorder, since obsessions almost always accompany compulsions. To define our terms, we have already described a compulsion in more detail as a repetitive striving to perform an unwelcome act, when that striving is laden with anxiety, but nevertheless is frequently irreversible. An obsession, which is the counterpoint of compulsion, is an idea which repetitively obtrudes upon conscious awareness as an objectively strange thought, as unwelcome as a compulsive striving, and also fraught with anxiety, when that idea symbolically represents a regressive urge which is derived from that individual's infancy.

To return for a moment to normalcy, giving our preoccupation (or obsession?) with the normative its due, we see the obsession of a normal child with the idea "I will be good now," or at a somewhat more mature level, "I will not think impure thoughts." Such an obsession appeared in a young woman from a rigidly religious, sexually suppressive background, who kept her antifertility pills in her bureau drawer on top of her Bible. To wrestle occasionally with the obsessive fear of death or of committing homicide, can be within normal limits in wending our way in today's difficult times, and may be of definite protective value to other automobilists, pedestrians and cocktail partygoers as well.

The word "obsession" is also used as a lay term to express a recurrent thought which has major compelling value. In the summary to the chapter on the Sense of Justice, we use the term obsession in its lay sense.

In the consultation room, one sees obsessions with death or violence. A middle-aged woman, who had originally complained of depression, gradually documented the story of her fear that she had poisoned some innocent strangers: At a country cottage which she owned but rented out for the winter, she had left small sacks of rat poison, exactly one per drawer, in precisely the farthest leftward corner. Fearing that the active ingredient, which is toxic to man only if it is eaten in generous helpings, would have harmed her tenants, she followed the obituary column of the weekly country newspaper, to be sure that they had not died of its effect. She also called the Health Department, the medical editor of a major newspaper, the Department of Pharmacology at a medical college and other similar sources, in order to "make assurance double sure," on this item.

In addition, she had been calling her husband several times a day at his office to be certain that he had not suffered an injury in traffic, and that his general health was still adequate. After some exposure to these calls, her husband had worked out an approach by which his secretary would answer for him by responding to her grave questions with a continuously varying pattern of well-modulated positive clucks. This secretary was well qualified to answer, for she was keeping abreast of her employer's current condition while having a discreet affair with him.

Another patient was obsessed with the thought that her husband would commit suicide, which would result in bringing her immeasureable grief and a large inheritance. She incessantly observed him for covert signs of impeding self-destruction, causing him to feel that social and sexual intercourse with her was rather more an examination than an exchange. She would flee from her obsession and its anxieties every Saturday night, by ingesting substantial amounts of alcohol and taking sleeping medication as a chaser, with which she achieved both unconsciousness and immobility until late the next morning. Her weekly "passing out cold" as she put it, served the purpose both of relieving her of the full awareness of her concern over her husband's death, and also effecting, in her, a psychically deathly retribution for her idea. She complained of being a compulsive Saturday night addict, which was considered to be an objectively accurate description. But her compulsion, which was symptomatic of her disorder, did not end in her having the sleep portrayed by Juliet for the sake of Romeo *every* Saturday, for she voluntarily abstained from alcohol and other drugs on several weekend occasions, in order to be more alert for receptions in relation to her daughter's wedding.

Similarly, her obsession with her husband's suicide, and her compulsion to inspect him with this thought in mind, did not impinge upon all of her conscious hours, nor did it continually occupy all of her waking moments with him.

Without elaborating on the psychodynamics of the obsessive compulsive disorder, as this has been described with expertness and great clarity in psychiatric references that are readily available (42, 71, 69) we shall describe some of the characteristics of the objective behavior of the person who has the compulsions which are a part of the Obsessive Compulsive Disorder, or trait. The individual who labors under the influence of such a compulsion is not a slave to the domination of his compulsion throughout his every moment, awake or asleep. Just as the fear of an ever present danger can be put aside for periods of time, so, too, can a compulsion. He may consciously control his behavior part of the time, or when he finds other avenues for his mental energies, he may control his compulsive behavior most of the time. In addition, the nature of the expression of the compulsive behavior may be altered by conscious or other forces that are brought to bear upon the compulsive act. In the case of an individual who felt compelled to touch buttocks, he became a collector of sculpture, affording him the opportunity for a moment to stroke his bronzes, thereby improving their texture. In a similar change of direction of the individual's motivations, a compulsive alcoholic may become an inexorable gourmand, stuffing himself with food instead of drink.

The compulsive striving, or the symptomatic compulsion, is not present in consciousness during every moment of conscious awareness. Nor does such an aware individual feel consciously coerced to heed every detail of this striving, wherever there is the physical opportunity to carry out the compulsion. A basic dynamic explanation for this phenomenon is this: A compulsion tends to remain in the unconscious mind at all times, only to appear in the conscious area when there is both a weakening of the repressive forces which abet its retention in the unconscious, and also a strengthening of expressive forces which aid its emergence into the conscious. Secondly, again drawing on our knowledge of general psychodynamics, since the compulsive motivation, or wish, is a primitive one and one that is psychologically prohibited, it has a tendency to emerge in a form which is distorted, by tending, when it is possible, to appear in a more permissible pattern.

In the specific case of compulsive alcoholics, a distinguished expert (45) describes several varieties of manifestation of this compulsion, or of the reaction to it. In one form, the alcoholic cannot abstain from drinking, but is able to control the amount of alcohol he takes. On the other hand, another group can abstain totally for days or even weeks, but if they begin drinking again, they cannot control the amount of intake. They may also suffer withdrawal symptoms when they ingest little alcohol or none. "During the period between drinking bouts, they may not suffer from an overwhelming compulsion, as the situation is entirely different.

> While there is either overt or covert accumulation of tension, there are none of the symptoms displayed in the interrupted bout, and the alcoholic does not show any signs of 'needing' alcohol. After a while, however, he wants to feel 'different' and he knows of no other way to achieve this than through alcohol."

Thus we have seen that the legislative and legal significance of a compulsion differs significantly from the psychological meaning of this symptom. Under the law which concentrates on the conscious characteristics of the actor who performs a specific act, no significant standing is given to the vast bulk of that actor's unconscious mind, which we know from psychology to dominate the conscious. In addition, our legislation and our courts have not yet assimilated the clinical knowledge that an individual who suffers from a compulsive disorder can, in certain specific ways, control his compulsion, or alter its expression.

CHAPTER 7

THE SENSE OF JUSTICE

SUMMARY

The sense of justice is a universal, psychosocial, obsessional idea that is imposed on the individual in the course of his becoming civilized. Its rules and laws are rooted in history, it becomes manifest in the preadolescent child when that child becomes sufficiently mature to conceive of social abstractions, and it derives its principal emotional energy from the strivings seen in the young child to make a family.

The sense of justice is composed of a doctrine, a concept and a striving. The doctrine of justice is the recorded code of justice whose origins are fairness as command, fairness as contract, utilitarianism and divine command. The concept of justice is the child's expression of his personal code of justice in society, as suggested by Piaget and brilliantly tested and organized by Kohlberg, Hoffman and Tapp. The striving for justice is regulated by the superego, which has two faces. The negative superego is harsh, promoting masochism, producing the "Injustice Collector," accounting for poetic justice and giving license to retribution for crime. The positive superego or constructive superego encourages the character traits of orderliness and affectionateness, promoting the harmonious socialization that fosters the consensus and reciprocity which are essential to the highest level of moral justice.

THE SENSE OF JUSTICE

"Justice is one of the most highly respected notions of our spiritual universe. All men — religious believers and non-believers, traditionalists and revolutionaries — invoke justice, and none dare disavow it. The search for justice inspires both the objurgations of the Hebrew prophets and the reflections of the Greek philosophers. It is invoked to protest the established order as well as to justify its overthrow." (75)

The sense of justice is a universal psychosocial "obsession" which consists of three parts. The first part is developed in the mind of the preadolescent child. The second part is rooted in history and the third part is incorporated into the psychology of the human community.

The basis of the sense of justice which appears within the historical framework of legislation and the law has been formulated for the rational or the reasonable man, by the cognitive or the knowing and learning man. But the pure reason of such men is not the only origin of the sense of justice. An additional origin of this sense is derived from our society. The rational and logical procedures of our sense of justice must be adapted to a society that is continually changing, even changing its idea of the nature of justice as a usufruct of the rights of man. For in this society, man's rights, and to a far lesser extent his responsibilities, have ever been pressing forward. Thus both the sense of justice and the law, which must be stable, may never stand fully still.

Lastly, this combination of the rational with the social sense of justice would be as blind as a sculpture of Astraea, the goddess of justice, unless it goes beyond orderly logic and the sometimes disorderly community, to its third part. This part consists of those emotional and nonrational strivings within the individual's subself or unconscious, which not only give form to his sense of justice, but also serve as their own enforcer, by means of generating the human conscience, which in turn gives license to retribution.

The sense of justice, which may be defined at this point as an internalized psychological formula for social utility, is thus composed of three major parts. The first part is the rational portion, which is based on precedent, history and ancient lore. The second part is societal, derived from human interactions within an ever changing community. The third part is emotional and nonrational.

It develops in the mind of the young child, being generated from those internalized psychological forces which are related to man's conscience, and which primarily account for the relationship between legal penalty and societal retribution.

Keeping in mind the fact that these three parts function in a dynamic relationship with each other, I should like to describe them separately, calling the rational portion the Doctrine of Justice, the societal portion the Concept of Justice, and the emotional part the Striving for Justice. Since this emotional striving has the ability to overcome each or both of the other two portions we shall describe it first.

THE STRIVING FOR JUSTICE

While in the next section we shall describe the rational doctrine of justice that has been enunciated by some of the great rational philosophers and lawmakers of history, and in the last section we shall touch upon the concept of justice as uncovered in experiments by rational-cognitive psychologists, we shall now map the anatomy of the striving for justice that is generated within the emotions of man. This striving has an emotional component which may easily overwhelm reason and distort logical behavior. But on the other hand, we shall show that this striving also can enrich the life of an individual who is a member of a civilized society, and at the same time help to elevate his level of morality.

I shall discuss these emotional strivings from the point of view of superego development. The Superego has two sides — the harsh or the negative superego and the benign or positively constructive superego. The negative superego promotes masochism and gives license to retribution, while its other side, the positive or benign superego, contributes to the traits of orderliness, affectional behavior and harmonious socialization.

The Negative Superego

A well informed man, and probably the reasonable man of American law — or his English counterpart "the man on the Clapham omnibus" — is already familiar with the notion of the superego. The superego is usually called strict, demanding, severe or even tyrannical, reminiscent of the image of the New England deacon, or the orthodox Jewish father as depicted by his son the novelist. Some psychoanalysts have even described the superego as "raging against the ego" or as "sadistic." Even that gentle philosopher of psychoanalytic psychology, Erikson, says that it "may achieve a triumph of deprecation" (58).

The superego is usually described as the controlling portion of the personality. In summary, the strict superego is formed from the solution of the Oedipus complex. When the child at the age of about 6 or 7 is frustrated by being unable to possess the full attentions and energies of his parent of the opposite sex, he is impelled by a bio-psychological mechanism to rectify this frustration. He solves the problem by means of imitation, introjection (or internalization) and identification (or becoming basically similar to another individual in one or more respects). (Imitation is conscious, introjection is partially conscious, and identification is unconscious.) In the case of a boy who cannot completely possess his mother, these psychological dynamics result in his identifying with his father figure, who does — as the child fantasies it — completely possess her. At least in fantasy, this identification solves the problem that is posed by his wish to possess mother.

In this process of mastering the Oedipus complex, he internalizes other fantasy features than this right to possession. These other introjects or internalizations include authority and a code of morality, which in turn include the right to punish transgressions, just as the child is customarily punished by the authority figure in the family. Perhaps because he is a little boy, too young to conceive the relation between the apparent and the real, he takes his child's eye view of father's authority as reality, thus arrogating to himself, particularly if his father figure is authoritarian or punitive, a sense of authority that is severe, rigid or even hostile. While other factors may account for these findings (58), we shall use this scheme to explain the strict authority of the harsh or the negative superego.

The Injustice Collector

Having gained this tyrannical authority in the core of his personality, an individual proceeds to exercise it in ways which under some conditions may be counter-productive of happiness. One type of individual character who uses this authoritarian superego to tyrannize his striving for happiness is the Injustice Collector. The Injustice Collector is a term that is associated with the names of Bergler and Meerloo, two sophisticated psychoanalysts who write with wit and verve (11). In Bergler and Meerloo's hands, the injustice collector is a common but pathological type of character, whose bursts of unwise anger often "leave an observer utterly perplexed in his wonder asking, 'what got into him that time?.' "

"What got into him" usually has little or nothing to do with the time, the place, or the person involved in the injustice collector's tantrum. Actually, he is paying off an old score, and using an innocent bystander in order to do so. The neurotic habitually re-enacts the anachronistic conflicts of childhood during his adult life, with people in his contemporary circle unknowingly playing the parts of the villains of his past. When, for example, a habitual injustice collector raises an unreasonable row in a restaurant because he wants steak and the last steak has just been served to someone else, he is unconsciously casting his helpless waiter in the role of the cruel mother of childhood, who capriciously denied him what he wanted."

Laboring under the duty to supply his personality with repeated dosages of mental pain and humiliation, the injustice collector becomes a specialist in exhibiting a spurious sort of aggression, which Bergler and Meerloo call pseudoaggression. Pseudoaggression is a variety of aggression that is appropriate in the nursery, but is as inappropriate to the normal preadolescent, or to the older individual, as would be the raw material of the Oedipal Complex. Its purpose is the opposite of real aggression, as real aggression is often designed to protect or to enhance the subject. Pseudoaggression's unconscious motivation is self damaging, for it is always bound both to stop short of success and also to prepare the scene for a drama of victimization and self-pity. A concise table from Bergler and Meerloo (11) details the ludic features of the injustice collector's pseudoaggression (Table 5).

Unlicensed Poetic Justice and the License for Retribution

The injustice collector is a prime example of the vengeful superego turned inward upon oneself. He is the prosector for

Table 5. The Injustice Collector

Normal Aggression	*Neurotic Aggression (pseudo-aggression)*
1. Used only in self-defense	1. Used indiscriminately when an infantile pattern is repeated with an innocent bystander.
2. Object of aggression is a "real" enemy.	2. Object of aggression is a "fantasied" or artifically created enemy.
3. No accompanying feeling of guilt.	3. Feeling of guilt always present.
4. Dosis: Amount of aggression discharged corresponds to provocation.	4. Dosis: Least provocation — greatest aggression.
5. Aggression always used to harm enemy.	5. Pseudo-aggression often used to provoke masochistic pleasure expected from enemy's retaliation, or to refute superego accusation of masochistic passivity.
6. Timing: Ability to wait until enemy is vulnerable.	6. Timing: Inability to wait, since pseudo-aggression is used as a defense against inner reproach of psychic masochism.
7. Not easily provoked.	7. Easily provoked.
8. Element of infantile game absent; no combination with masochistic and defensively "sadistic" feelings; the only feeling is that a necessary through disagreeable job has to be performed.	8. Element of infantile game present, combined with masochistic and defensively "sadistic" excitement, usually repressed.
9. Success expected.	9. Defeat unconsciously expected.

The Injustice Collector's type of neurotic aggression, or pseudo-aggression. From Bergler, E., and Meerloo, J.A.M.: *Justice and Injustice,* New York, Grune and Stratton, 1963, page 27.

"poetic justice," when poetic justice is succeeded by retribution. Retribution resembles poetic justice in that the punishment in both modes of reaction is considered just punishment. But in retribution the punishment is not executed through a subtle or an overt interplay between the offender and the victim, because in retribution the punishment is decreed by the community at large, and is executed by that community's impersonal system of justice.

The fantasy of poetic justice, as compelling as the fate music of the opera, is as familiar to the average man as the dramatic upshot of one's receiving his just deserts. This fantasy, described so well by the late Edmund Bergler (11, p. 155) calls for a specific type of pre-ordained retribution, in which the villain, at some time in the future, will suffer exactly the unhappy end to which he subjected his innocent victim. Like the audience in the opera, the community knows full well what is transpiring in this fateful drama, even though the actors as we see them on the stage, and real persons in real life who act out this sequence, are unconscious of its significance.

But retribution is a more social expression of our individual psychology than is poetic justice. Retribution is the revenge which is imposed on an offender by the community, at the bidding of the collective superego of that community. By means of retribution, each individual is able to pool the harsh demands of his negative superego with those of his fellow citizens, so that this collective pool not only becomes more powerful than the individual's wishes, but also becomes more nearly impersonal (2).

At about the turn of this century, the French sociologist Emile Dirkheim proposed that we have a collective conscience, a structure of the community's personality which recognizes justice and proposes appropriate redress for injustice. Similar to the individual conscience, the collective conscience is at the ready to mete out punishment. Psychodynamically, in retribution our aggressive feelings take a permissible outlet, affording the collective conscience a sense of relief when appropriate punishment is carried out. Thus we feel relieved when the guilty one is fined, imprisoned, or until 1968, executed, so that he has "paid his debt to society."

But in that small portion of the conscience which is unconscious, as is the greatest part of the superego, even more powerful strivings must be reckoned with. That inclination which is present to some degree in every man toward original sin, unfettered freedom or the gratification of the instincts (which are different names of the striving for pleasure that we have arranged in the historical order of their being recorded) finds its fellow in some way and to some degree, in the offender against justice. Some small and well concealed part of the individual, and of the community, thus indentifies with the violent or the prohibited act of the offender.

Then, if the offender receives punishment at the hands of the community, the citizenry is relieved of its fantasies of committing violent or prohibited acts. In this picture, the sacrifice of a single and well publicized wrongdoer's property, liberty or life will relieve a large number of law abiding persons (3) from the anxiety that is associated with their fantasies of wrongdoing. With the sharing of this relief, the license for retribution is granted.

So much for the punitive superego turned inward on the injustice collector and on the villain in a case of poetic justice, and the punitive superego turned outward, giving license for retribution.

> "The problem of 'man in search of a target' is familiar not only from clinical observations and the daily life of the child, but — as Freud had seen — from the vicissitudes of our social organization itself. One might say that social conflict is exploited by the manipulation of the masses to provide the individual group member with an enemy whom he eagerly accepts as a target of aggression, thus using social tension for the displacement of individual tension" (39).

Now let us examine the benign side of the superego.

The Constructive Superego

The constructive superego, when it exerts its energies in a positive direction within the community, is largely responsible for the character traits of orderliness, affection and harmonious socialization of the individual, and thus promotes morality and justice in the community. But before we show how this comes about, let us first define a character trait.

> A trait of character develops as a substitute for a forbidden wish. For example, when a child of about 1 1/2 years begins the anal stage of his development, one may readily see in him the signs of the instinct and the wish to dirty and disorder. Within a few months, however, he grows to place an apparent value on cleanliness and order. Probably two vectors converge on this one instinctual drive.

One is the negative superego, related to the stern command "NO, NO!," which is succeeded by what Ferenczi called "Sphincter Morality" (21). The other is the child's pleasure in accepting the invitation to be like the parent, who praises and rewards the child for being "good." Cleanliness and order, as the child develops and interrelates, grow beyond the diameter of his diaper and crib. Order becomes a "good" way of relating to others without the dirty disorder of free fecal soiling. Thus the child may become clean and orderly as a substitute for the forbidden wish to soil.

The character trait of orderliness is an "important requirement of civilization" (30) and as we see in the last section, is an important stage in the development of morality (95). Both the malign and the benign superego contribute to the formation of orderliness, but the ideal superego gives a bonus for order, in essence saying "Good" instead of "No, No!"

The trait of affectionateness also has a similar type of evolution. A child's wish to love intensively, as we have seen with the Oedipal wish, is frustrated by prohibitions which come from the negative or the hostile superego. [The force of this frustration is seen by the power of the universal taboo against incest. "The strength of the incestuous wishes can still be detected behind the prohibition against them" (29).] But with the achievement of maturity, the individual may continue to demonstrate this wish, not by exuberant eroticism (which is prohibited for socially mature individuals) but instead by being affectionate within his social group. Freud wrote (30) "People give the name 'love' to the relation between a man and a woman whose genital needs have led them to found a family; but they also give the name 'love' to the positive feelings between parents and children and between the brothers and sisters of a family, although we are obliged to describe this as 'aim-inhibited love' or 'affection.' Love with an inhibited aim was in fact originally fully sensual love, and it is still in man's unconscious."

This aim-inhibited love *is* affection, which can be expressed in many social directions beyond the family. Bonds of affection can reach beyond one's extended family, past the band of brothers which makes up one's sociocultural group. Affection can link large numbers of individuals into larger social groups. This is one method by which the constructive superego encourages the growth of harmonious socialization.

The positive superego, which we have designated as the constructive superego, thus promotes orderliness, affectionateness and harmonious socialization. Orderliness in the little group of which the child is a major member — his family — is developed as a character trait which replaces his innate urge to disorderly soiling. As the child's group grows larger, the trait of orderliness is extended to function within his larger group — our society — in the form of community order. With great numbers of children and adults undergoing this process, a community will develop its own trait of orderliness as a feature of that community's traits.

In a similar fashion, affectionateness grows up as a trait of character which supersedes a wish for intense individual love. Affection radiates from the individual to members of the family and to the community, and can be reflected back from them. This exchange of affection nurtures the development of harmonious socialization by impelling the individual toward a form of gentle caring for numbers of his fellows, as opposed to his intense individual love for a few individuals. This gentle and affectionate caring provides the emotional energy for harmonious socialization.

With harmonious socialization, a durable type of social interrelationship is developed among members of a community. The exchange of energies by these members is associated with their collaboration at work. Under these circumstances of socialization, this collaboration yields a sense of mutual respect, which is a feature of the highest level of morality.

THE DOCTRINE OF JUSTICE

The doctrine of justice is the formal explication of justice which appears in our rules, codes and statutes. We shall describe this doctrine under four of its major categories — as a command to be fair, then as a contract to be fair, thence under utilitarianism and finally as Divine Will.

1. Fairness as Command

Rooted in ancient lore, the doctrine of justice as a command to be fair has become a shibboleth of the Western world. Not long after the invention of a written language, judges in Egypt were told "regard him whom thou knowest as one whom thou knowest not" while in Deuteronomy we see, "ye shall not respect persons in judgment, but ye shall hear the small as well as the great" (I:17). In a powerful passage, Moses says, "Ye shall diligently keep the Commandments of the Lord your God, and his testimonies, and his statutes, which he has commanded thee. And thou shalt do that which is right and good in the sight of the Lord" (Deuteronomy VI:17-18). The Golden Rule in its original form, was "Do not unto others as thou wouldst not be done by," its style seeming legalistic today. Similar to this rule is the categorical imperative of Immanuel Kant, "Act on principles which you would see universally adopted."

But this universal rule of justice, devaluating the special qualities and needs of the individual, is being modified without losing the basic universality of its approach. Thus we see in Sidgwick's axioms of justice, "Whatever action of us he judges to be right for himself, he implicitly judges to be right for all similar persons in similar circumstances." A more highly individualized application, which is consistent with modern law, is stated in Clarke's rule of equity, "whatever I judge reasonable or unreasonable, that another should do for me; that by the same judge must I declare reasonable that in the like case do for him" (32). Thus, by introducing the significance of similar persons, similar circumstances and therefore similar cases, we begin to move from the command to do absolute justice, toward the command to follow a more relative justice, a justice that is personalized. Even farther into the individualization of justice is the proposal by Del Vecchio that *alteritas,* or the idea that another human being is an *alter ego,* so that we all differ, is at the basis of the Golden Rule (5).

2. Fairness as Contract

The doctrine of fairness which is less of a command and more of a contract, where that contract is agreed upon in a democracy, was foreshadowed by Aristotle in his definition of pleonexia. Aristotle wrote that justice requires us to refrain from pleonexia, which consists in gaining advantage by seizing another's property, another's reward or office, or denying his due, fulfillment of a promise, repayment of a debt, proper respect, etc. Pleonexia is a wrongful act which is generally similar to a tort in common law. But in the times that shortly preceded the industrial revolution, the notion of fairness as a form of justice that is derived from a social contract was elaborated by Locke, Rousseau and Kant. Rosseau commented on the general will or *volonté generale,* to say that governmental action was unjust unless it conformed to the general will. Rousseau also felt that society was corrupt, but that children were originally unspoiled in nature, a concept to which we shall return in the next section. Free, rational and equal persons, writes Kant, define the terms of their association in the form of a contract. They agree in essence to regulate all further agreements, to specify the kinds of social cooperation that are permissible, and to set forth those forms of government that can be established (81).

In this contractarian form of justice, Rousseau noted that the volonté generale may change in its character. The current character of stated public aspirations tends to be social, deep-seated, unselfish and non-exploitative (68). But it seems to be changing more slowly than was expected in his revolutionary times by Rousseau, for Justice Holmes wrote in 1922, "If a thing has been practiced for two hundred years by common consent, it will need a strong case for the XIV Amendment to affect it (88).

Within the frame of contractarian justice, we have developed a major policy which governs the character of the law. This policy is the rule of law. The rule of law, as opposed to the rule of man, is composed of four principles (32).

1. No one can judge his own case.
2. Disputes are settled without force.
3. Coercive powers of law are not unlimited.
4. Lawmakers are themselves subject to the law.

3. Utility

A third major definition of justice which has been incorporated into our codes is the definition of justice as utility. Utility describes the principles by which social means produce social ends. Thus Hutcheson in 1725, in *An Enquiry Concerning Moral Good and Evil,* wrote that "that action is best which promotes the greatest happiness in the greatest numbers, and that action is worst which in like manner occasions the deepest misery for the largest numbers" (81). But radically distinguished from its quest for happiness, another utilitarian approach concerns the integrity and therefore the survival of the commonwealth. In this light, the existence of a stable legal system has public utility, in which our particular individual acts of obedience are instrumental to building up the stability of the system as a whole, while our individual acts of disobedience are destructive of this common cause (Ladd). Each particular act by each citizen, therefore, builds up or tears down the community, each act to its own extent. Thus utility promotes both happiness and the stability which encourages survival — happiness and stability being two phenomena of human life which can coexist successfully in varying intergrades, or which under special circumstances may be mutually destructive.

The names in the 18th century of P.J.A. Feuerbach, John Stuart Mill and Jeremy Bentham are the most outstanding of those which are associated with utility. Thus Mill wrote that justice is a term for certain classes of moral values, namely those which concern the essentials of social life such as security. This utilitarian view is reflected by Roscoe Pound (87) who wrote that "justice as applied to law is not an individual virtue, nor is it the ideal relation among men. It is merely such an adjustment of relations and ordering of conduct as will make the goods of existence go round as far as possible with the least friction and waste" (87).

Bentham, a brilliantly persuasive lawyer and international legislative consultant, was concerned with happiness as the principal end result of his utility doctrine, although he failed to define his term by writing "what happiness is, every man knows." Bentham is also associated with the notion of the Felicific Calculus (a term which delights my students as much as describing the evil mind, or mens rea of criminal law, as 'blackness of heart'). Applying the felicific calculus, a rational and cognitive man will calculate the amount of happiness he would achieve through a certain act, against the amount of unhappiness that would ensue on performing that act. Were he able, like Astraea, the goddess of justice, to hold the scales of justice in his hand, he would weigh the pleasureable versus the miserable consequences of his act, to make his logical choice, without any modification of his measurements by his early religious training or by the psychic strivings of his personality.

But despite his times (1748-1832) Bentham was a psychological hedonist, along the lines which were clearly drawn by Sigmund Freud one hundred years later, (59) when Freud showed that pleasure determines conduct. The way to improve human conduct, wrote Bentham, is to get greater pleasure from moral conduct than from immoral conduct. The individual's achievement of pleasure thus produces group pleasure by the utility principle.

Not only did Bentham recognize a drive toward pleasure, but he also conceptualized a sense of mental pain, just as we use the term "pain and suffering" in modern law. This pain was a feature of Bentham's four sanctions, as he believed that pain is the coercive or binding force which is incurred by disobedience of a sanction. (A sanction in ethics is an authority, such as the golden rule, which supports a moral activity, while on the other hand a sanction in law is a coercion, such as a penalty, which is linked to the violation of a law, being designed to enforce that law.) Bentham used 'sanction' to mean a source of pain or pleasure. Bentham stated that pain results from disobedience of the physical sanction to tend the body, and that the moral sanction demands obedience at the cost of public censure, and the pain which results from violation of the religious sanction is effective to the extent to which an individual believes in a supreme being and a life after death. Violation of "political" sanctions, consisting of violation of statutes, is a criminal act that is punishable through the courts (8).

Returning to his felicific calculus, Bentham writes that virtue is "the sacrifice of a less interest to a greater, of a momentary to a more durable, of a doubtful to a certain interest." While on vice he writes, "Vice may be defined to be a miscalculation of chances, a mistake in estimating the value of pleasure and pains. It is false moral arithmetic." And as to crime, we see the rule which prevails today in many of the United States — that a criminal intent — or the evil mind — is required to constitute a crime, in a pungent Benthamism. "All the several pleas and excuses," he wrote, "which protect the committer of a forbidden act from punishment . . . may be reduced to a single consideration — the want or defect of will, [and to the principle] that to constitute a crime, there must be first, a vitious will" (38). This in turn, harks back to the Roman code of intent as a necessary feature of the crime, which is preserved in current American law as the mens rea doctrine, from "Actus non facit reum, nisi mens rea," or, "the act does not make one guilty, without an evil mind."

4. Creator Versus Creature

The separation of church from state, drawn by a bold stroke in the American colonies, and radically proclaimed by the people of other great land masses a sesquicentennium later, is an innovation in the long history of justice. But in the times of Plato, who said that justice is the supreme virtue which harmonizes all the other virtues, and that all individual virtues were reproductions of the virtues of the state (77), the state was considered to be guided by the gods. In his search for a rational relationship between the soul, the state and the cosmos, Plato's vision of the absolute good (the goods are the products of existence) was possible exclusively through a special and mystic experience, which only a few can obtain, and then solely by intercession of divine grace (50).

From the time of Ptolemy, about 150 A.D., who proved that the earth was the center of the universe, with the sun, the planets and the constellations revolving around the earth, through that of Copernicus, about 1500 A.D., who then proved that the sun was the center of the universe, the relationship between an anthropomorphic Divine Creator and the creature man was the preponderant feature of man's justice. In this epicycle, the closer that one approaches godliness, it was propounded, the closer may man grasp justice. In the 13th century, Bracton, who was both a cleric and judge (88) wrote:

"Justice, then, is a constant and perpetual will to award to each his right, the definition of which may be understood in two manners; in one manner as it is in the Creator, in another as it is in the creature. And if it be understood as it is in the Creator, that is in God, all things are plain, since justice is the disposal of God, which orders rightly and disposes rightfully in all things."

In this period, the dichotomy between Creator and creature was exemplified by the distinction between two forms of justice, moral justice and jural justice. Moral justice was defined by laws which were "given," hence unchanging and unchangeable. Being given in this fashion, they were known naturally to normal adults. But on the other hand, the creature was governed also by jural justice, which was delimited by the laws which were made and enforced by the state. Of the two, the natural or divine law was infinitely preponderant.

In the philosophy of Locke, the idea of "justice, or the thought of a good and rational order," constituted the center of reference for man. Locke proposed that (a) an infinitely powerful, infinitely wise God exists and ordains all things related to man, (b) the Almighty has given man faculties such that he can, if he makes good use of his capacities for being rational and free, discover the laws of the order thus ordained, and act according to these laws." And it must be noted that this Judeo-Christian ethic has been remarkably persistent in history.

Legal sanctions were imposed upon those hapless creatures who faltered in their steps toward divine grace. Thus eschewing Hume's dictum that justice is a cautious virtue (81) were certain statutes of the colony of Massachusetts. In the *Capitall Lawes Established Within the Jurisdiction of Massachusetts* of 1642, we see that "If any man, after legal conviction, shall have or worship any God, other than the Lord God, he shall be put to death." This citation was noted appropriately by a contemporary law professor at Harvard (88), in Cambridge, where a court session is often opened with the bailiff declaiming, "God save the Commonwealth of Massachusetts."

Over a century later, the penal reform law of 1778 in England drawn by Blackstone and two others, prescribed the treatment (89) of those who had fallen from grace:

> "By sobriety, cleanliness, and medical assistance, by a regular series of labour, by solitary confinement during the intervals of work, and by due religious instruction to preserve and amend the health of the unhappy offenders, to inure them to habits of industry, to guard them from pernicious company, to accustom them to serious reflection and to teach them both the principles and practice of every Christian and moral duty."

On being confined in such an institution, the prisoner was then adjured to reflect on his deviation from moral justness. By such reflection, he could enter a state of repentance. It is for precisely this reason that some of our prisons are still called penitentiaries.

In an overview, I cannot agree with Leibniz, who wrote that "the notions of right and of justice are still far from clear, despite the fact that the clearest of writers have written about them." Instead, this brief history of the rational philosophy of the doctrine of justice, scanning four components of this doctrine — fairness as command, fairness as contract, utility, and divine will, leads to a clear conclusion. This conclusion is that philosophy has foreshadowed psychology in our study of the doctrine of justice. In the sections on social psychology and individual psychology we demonstrate this to be the case with the remaining components of the sense of justice.

THE CONCEPT OF JUSTICE

As contrasted to the doctrine of justice which we described in the previous section, the concept of justice is a socio-psychological concept which the individual may consciously express after it has formed in his mind as a result of his moral development. While the definition of moral development by some legislators may refer to acceptable sexual practices as opposed to unacceptable ones, social psychologists take a broader view. They write that moral development is the development of moral behavior. Moral behavior, in turn, is behavior which a social group currently defines as "good" or as "right," and for which that group administers sanctions, of which some are statutory. This development and behavior reflects values: "Moral values are beliefs concerning what is good and what is right that are shared within a social group. Among these beliefs, there are more *thou shalt nots,* than *thou shalts*" (60).

Now the moral development of the child has been studied under the aegis of three different philosophies, the first two being radically opposed to each other, and the third being an accommodation of its two predecessors. These philosophical theories, which are formally given scientific and even elegant names, are referred to by professionals in the social sciences as (1) Original Sin, (2) Pristine Purity and (3) The Unprogrammed Computer.

In the theory of original sin, the child is viewed as a bundle of biological drives, with these drives striving in the main toward pure pleasure, alloyed perhaps with other drives that are also incompatible with civilized society. Beginning at the age of about six, the child's drives may then slowly become tamed, more mature in expression, and even enriched by the sublimation of these drives into socially laudable traits. In the second theory, that of pristine purity, it is not the child who is evil, because of his drives over which he exerts little control. In this philosophy the child is inherently pure, while it is society that is corrupt. As enunciated by Rousseau, and studied by his follower Jean Piaget at the Rousseau Institute in Geneva, the society of adults is a particularly corrupting influence, which should be minimized during the child's early formative years. In the third theory, that of the unprogrammed computer, or to leap backward from this technologic age to the waxen tablet or the *tabula rasa,* the child is neither purely sinful nor completely pure. The child is instead infinitely ductile and malleable, being constantly shaped by the social learning into which he is pressed by his environment (43).

The "original sin" theory as it engenders development has received major support from a recent but classic experiment in social psychology, which studied the refusal to repudiate an authority's immoral command. Milgram at Yale, in a study of obedience, tested about 1000 male subjects aged 20 through 50, of unskilled labor through professional socio-educational status, for their obeying or disobeying an order to give a dangerous electric shock to another man (67). The first study was done in Milgram's laboratory at Yale, while the second was done in a marginally respectable and somewhat run down commercial building in downtown Bridgeport, unkown to the subjects except by an advertisement for the "Research Associates of Bridgeport," a title which was concocted for this experiment.

In both series, the subjects were told that they were to participate in an experiment to show the effect of punishment on memory, the punishment consisting of electric shocks. They were instructed to operate a machine which had 30 levers, each marked with its own voltage in increments of 15 volts, with prominent labels reading from "Slight Shock" to "DANGER — Severe Shock." The subjects were each given an actual shock of 45 volts to convince them of the authenticity of the procedure. However, the machine did not truly deliver any shock at all to the experimental "victim." The "victim" was trained to make responses so that at apparent 75 volts he would begin to grunt and moan. At apparent 150 volts, he demands to be let out of the experiment, and at apparent 180 volts he cries out that he can no longer stand the pain. He then commences to bang on the wall, etc. At apparent 300 volts, he refuses to supply any further answers to the simple memory test,

> "The victim indicates no discomfort until the 75-volt shock is administered, at which time there is a light grunt in response to the punishment. Similar reactions follow the 90- and 105-volt shocks, and at 120 volts the victim shouts to the experimenter that the shocks are becoming painful. Painful groans are heard on administration of the 135-volt shock, and at 150 volts the victim cries out, 'Experimenter, get me out of here! I won't be in the experiment any more! I refuse to go on!' Cries of this type continue with generally rising intensity, so that at 180 volts the victim cries out, 'I can't stand the pain,' and by 270 volts his response to the shock is definitely an agonized scream. Throughout, he insists that he be let out of the experiment. At 300 volts the victim shouts in desperation that he will no longer provide answers to the memory test; and at 315 volts, after a violent scream, he reaffirms with vehemence that he is no longer a participant. From this point on, he provides no answers, but shrieks in agony whenever a shock is administered; this continues through 450 volts."

When the "victim" was in the same room 1 1/2 feet away, only 40% of the subjects continued to press the levers. When the victim was shocked only while touching an apparent electric plate, but the subject had to force the "victim's" hand on to the plate, 30% persisted in giving the punishment.

The subjects were not at all at ease during the procedure (p. 68).

> "One puzzling sign of tension was the regular occurrence of nervous laughing fits. In the first four conditions 71 of the 160 subjects showed definite signs of nervous laughter and smiling. The laughter seemed entirely out of place, even bizarre. Full-blown, uncontrollable seizures were observed for 15 of these subjects. On one occasion we observed a seizure so violently convulsive that it was necessary to call a halt to the experiment. In the post-experimental interviews subjects took pains to point out that they were not sadistic types and that the laughter did not mean they enjoyed shocking the victim."

But despite these outbursts, which a clinician would call explosions of affect, they continued to press the levers. Professor Milgram wrote, "the results, as seen and felt in the laboratory, are to this author disturbing." To me this is a shocking display of our low level of moral development when it is subjected to stress by authority.

But one may ask, is not moral development at a higher level among the able and mainly well-educated leaders of our successful corporations? "No" writes R. C. Baumhart (6), then a doctoral candidate at the Harvard Business School, who studied a quite respectable number of well placed executives. This observer noted that the Greek historian Polybius wrote, "At Carthage, nothing which results in profit is disgraceful." At the time of his survey, Baumhart wrote, Carthaginian morality still prevails in the industrial community. From similar observations and from clinical studies, which go far deeper into interpersonal behavior than can the laboratory, one finds a strong case for the persistence of primitive and savage strivings within the mind of civilized man.

In the remainder of this section, however, we shall emphasize the second philosophy of moral development, the theory of Pristine Purity, by giving some of the stimulating concepts of Jean Piaget, and then going on to the major contributions of Kohlberg at Harvard. Piaget, in his study on the "Moral Judgment of the Child" (76) indeed shows that he is a follower of Rousseau, when he notes that it is not the parents who are responsible for children's sense of justice, but that "the mutual respect and solidarity which holds among children is the sole source of the sense of justice" (p. 195). This definition of the sense of justice, harking back to the contractarian justice of Kant and Rousseau, consists of a concern for reciprocity and equality among individuals.

Piaget's experiments with children led him to describe two stages in the development of morality — the Stage of Constraint, and the Stage of Cooperation.

> In Piaget's first moral stage, which he also refers to as moral realism or as the morality of constraint, the child feels an obligation to comply with rules because they are sacred and unalterable. The child tends to conceive behaviors as totally right or totally wrong, and seems to feel that everyone views them in the way that he does. He judges the rightness or wrongness of an act on the basis of

magnitude of its consequences, the extent to which it conforms exactly to established rules, and whether or not it evokes punishment. He believes in "immanent justice" in which violations of social norms are followed by physical catastrophe, or by misfortunes that are willed by God or else by some inanimate object.

Piaget's second moral stage, the stage of cooperation, which he also calls autonomous morality or the stage of reciprocity, is reached at about the age of 6. The child comes to this moral stage at that age not merely because of maturation, but primarily because of the development of his cognitive concepts. Cognitive concepts are the individual's hypotheses, strategies and intentions which determine his behavior (62). In this second and more mature phase of morality, the child does not view rules as rigid and unchangeable, but instead as maintained and established by reciprocal social agreement. Rules are thus subject to modification in response to human needs or to other demands which the situation makes upon them. The child gives up his previous moral absolutism and recognizes a possible diversity of his view of others' concepts of right and wrong. These judgments of right and wrong are not dominated now by the consequences of the act, but by the intention of the actor. He does not conceive of punishment being immanent or impersonal. Instead of duty or obligation being the outcome of obedience, in this second stage, duty and obligation derive from reciprocating with others, conforming to expectations of one's peers, considering their present welfare, or expressing affection for their past affection and their favors. While punishment in the first stage had been expiatory, painful and arbitrarily administered by the authority, in this second stage punishment is reciprocally related to the crime or to the misdeed, examples being by restitution, or through direct retaliation by the victim (43).

These stimulating ideas and researches by Piaget and his collaborators have resulted in other cognitive psychologists, principally in this country, confirming and extending his work. The cognitive psychologist is primarily interested in ideas and feelings of which the subject is consciously aware. As an example in Piaget's approach, the mechanism of *assimilation* plays a basic role in development of the child's thought and behavior. *Assimilation* describes how the developing child perceives the similarities of new items and new concepts to old items and old concepts, in order to incorporate them into his hypotheses and strategies.

Neo-Piagetian psychologists have investigated the criteria of moral maturity in the developing individual, in order to delimit his consciously expressed concept of justice. These criteria, or attributes, which were formulated in general by Piaget, include the child's concept of intentions versus consequences, and the question of conformity to the expectations of one's young peers, as opposed to the imperative of obedience to adult authority.

> The other criteria of moral development which have been subjected to intensive study are (1) a shift from absolutism of moral perspective to relativism, as in a youngster seeing that right or wrong has different meanings in different circumstances to different people. (2) The progress from expiatory and authority administered punishment, to restitutive and reciprocal forms of punishment, as in a youngster believing that punishment should be reciprocally related to the misdeed through restitution. (3) The giving up of immanent justice — in which a supernatural force strikes the offender in retribution — for a punishment based in reality, administered by the real community (Hoffman).

Correlations were sought between these criteria of moral maturity and other features of the individual, such as his intelligence quotient, his social class, and the type of child rearing which he was being given.

Investigators found that a higher level of moral maturity, and thus a more developed concept of justice, was demonstrated in those children who had a higher intelligence quotient and who also came from a higher social class. The fact that the higher social classes have a generally higher IQ did not negate this conclusion, in one well controlled study. This showed that both those who were in the lowest sector by IQ and those in the highest sector by IQ, all within the upper social class group, showed a higher level of the moral criteria, or attributes of Piaget. Child rearing practices as revealed by interviews with parents and their children, did not have an influence on the child's moral maturity (43 p. 272).

But something more was necessary. Lawrence Kohlberg at Harvard studied a group of young people over the period of their childhood through their mature years, until the age of 28 (95). In addition, he and his collaborators, including Tapp (92), a highly articulate researcher, made cross cultural studies, including children in Greece, India, Italy, Japan and Denmark, as well as U.S. Whites and U.S. Blacks. Kohlberg set up ten hypothetical moral questions, or dilemmas, in which acts of obedience to rules, laws or commands of authority came into conflict with the needs or the welfare of other persons. He also asked some basic moral questions including "What is a rule?" "What is a law?" "Why should people follow rules?" "Why do you follow rules?" "What would happen if there were no rules?" "Are there times when it might be right to break a rule?"

The responses which children gave to Kohlberg's questions and dilemmas were then classified. At the lowest level of classification, a primary school child said that "a rule is not to run around, not to hit anybody, not to break anything" thereby indicating a Law Obeying morality. At the intermediate level, an 8th grade girl said of a rule, "It's a guideline to follow, well, you just follow it," indicating a Law Maintaining Morality. At the highest level, a bright male college student said that a rule "was a judgment or a standard arrived at pragmatically or morally, affecting, directing and/or compelling behavior" indicating a Law Making Morality. At the highest stage in this level, another college student said that a "rule ought to be obeyed for the benefit of everyone, and it makes everything easier actually, and easier to live with."

Kohlberg and his collaborators thus found that there were not two levels of moral maturity, but three. Kohlberg's second level — that of conventional morality — appeared at from 7 to 10 years of age. The third or highest level did not appear until the end of high school in his U.S. subjects and was not completed until they were about 25 years of age (Table 6).

Kohlberg's highest phase is more in keeping with the new morality of the twentieth century than is the superior level of the Rosseau-Piaget concepts. Kohlberg pictures a strong constitutionalism at this level of development, with an emphasis on procedural rules for reaching a consensus, and his highest stages accentuate the possibility of making a change in the law for rational purposes, or for purposes of social utility.

In the cross cultural studies by Tapp and her associates, children or different cultures took essentially the same positions on moral questions and justice. In the cultures they studied, "the essential purpose of rules was to order man's relationship in the world: to facilitate human interaction." These children from many different countries also seemed to agree, in their own language, that "without rules, man's natural evil would take over — anarchy, greed and

Table 6.   The Three Levels of Morality

Level I — Law Obeying or Preconventional Level

At the preconventional level the cultural labels of "good" and "bad" are interpreted in terms of physical consequences (e.g., punishment, reward, exchange of favors) or in terms of the physical power of those who enunciate the rules and labels.

Stage 1.   Physical Power

The Physical Power stage characteristically orients toward punishment, unquestioning deference to superior power and prestige, and avoidance of "bad" acts. Regardless of value, physical consequences determine goodness and badness.

Stage 2.   Instrumental Relativism

The Instrumental Relativism stage is basically hedonistic. Right action consists of that which instrumentally satisfies one's own needs and occasionally the needs of others. Elements of fairness, equality, and reciprocity are present, but interpreted pragmatically, not as a matter of loyalty, gratitude, or justice.

Level II — Law Maintaining or Conventional Level

The conventional level is characterized by active support of the fixed rules or authority in a society. Maintaining the expectations and rules of the family, group, or nation is valued in its own right.

Stage 3.   Good Boy

The interpersonal concordance or good-boy/good-girl stage orients toward pleasing others and gaining approval. There is conformity to stereotypical images of majority behavior. Also behavior is frequently judged by intention: "He means well" becomes important for the first time.

Stage 4.   Law and Order

The Law and Order stage is typified by doing one's duty (obeying fixed rules), showing respect for authority, and maintaining the given social order. Respect is earned by performing dutifully.

Level III — Law Making or Postconventional Level

The postconventional level is characterized by a clear effort toward autonomous moral principles with validity apart from the authority of the groups or persons who hold them and apart from individual identifications.

Stage 5.   Social Contract

The Social Contract stage has legalistic and utilitarian overtones; strong constitutionalism pervades. Right action is defined in terms of individual rights, critically agreed upon by the whole society. Awareness of the relativism of personal values is attended by an emphasis upon procedural rules for reaching consensus. The stress is on the legal point of view, but with the possibility of changing law in terms of rational, social utility rather than freezing it in terms of law and order.

Stage 6.   Universal Ethic

The Universal Ethic stage moves toward conscientious decisions of right based on principles that appeal to logical comprehensiveness, universality, and consistency. These principles are abstract and ethical; they include justice, the reciprocity and equality of human rights, and respect for individuals.

The Criteria of Moral Development, from Tapp, J. L. and Kohlberg, L.: Developing Senses of Law and Justice, *Journal of Social Issues, 27* Number 2, pp. 65-91, 1971.

violence would win out." "Without rules," said a Danish boy, "the whole world would be under chaos." According to older children, again transglobally, if rule and law failed, disorder and personal gain would prevail. In this vein, an Italian sixth grader said "Everyone would do what he wanted" while a more sophisticated Italian 8th grader explained, "Life would not have a logical direction."

Kohlberg's table of moral development, which we reproduce here, is well worth review, because of its sound experimental basis and its projection of clinical realism in firm, clear terms (Table 6).

Tapp and Kohlberg assert that traditional social education in the United States is frequently "both undemocratic and unconstitutional" and customarily encourages the child to be compliant with the predominant adult rules and attitudes of the particular social system. In place of this current approach, they make a plea for the socialization of children which will promote the development of a sense of justice by means of experience based activity involving resolution of conflicts, problem solving, participation in the making of decisions and role-taking opportunities.

Now we see that cognitive psychologists have tapped the concepts of justice of young persons, to show that the highest level of morality is not reached until well into the age of reproductive maturity, or in our country, far beyond the voting age. In our overview, we have progressed in our study of the sense of justice from the objurgative command of the ancient Hebrew prophets to heed the doctrine of justice as an ideal, to a highly objective investigation by the cognitive psychologists on the concept of justice in the real child and the large-as-life youngster of today's ambient culture, after we found an explanation for these socio-psychological phenomena in an examination of the inner psychology of the individual for those of his instincts and anxieties which create within him a positive striving for justice.

CONCLUSION

We can now say that the sense of justice is a psychosocial structure which is formed from the substance of the three pillars which support it. The first pillar is the force of precedent which is based on the history of our civilization, as it is encoded in our rules and our laws. The great force of this precedent was thought to be derived in earliest times from the will of supernatural forces, and later from the wish of an anthropomorphic God, as it has been inscribed through the wisdom of man. Derived from this wish, and seldom directly negating it, are the statutes which represent the collective will of the people. The historical force of this precedent shapes the boundaries within which an individual may work and within which he may love, at the same time as it gives the direction to the moral policies of our community. The development of every infant and adult is thus continually influenced by the precedent which has handed down the rules of justice.

The second pillar upon which justice rests is that development of the child which stimulates him to conceive of these rules of justice as abstractions which are not only generally valid, but which particularly govern him. To grasp the abstract idea of justice that is utilized by adults requires the apprehension of a rudimentary sense of justice which develops at about six years of age. In addition, the development of this grasp is made either firmer or weaker in the growing youngster by the behavior and the feelings of the adults who play the most significant roles in his rearing.

The third pillar of justice is the powerful influence of the superego. The superego is one of the regulating psychological structures in the character of the individual and is reflected in the nature of his civilization. In noting how the superego has both a harsh or punitive side, which is a limiting vector, and a benign side, which is a stimulating vector, I have shown how the superego effects a balance between these vectors to generate and maintain his individual sense of morality and his personal sense of justice.

Thus the *thou shalt nots* and the *thou shalts* of divine command and legislative precedent are developed in the individual in his current societal setting, when the biologic and conceptual maturation of the individual permits him to codify the strivings within his own superego.

BIBLIOGRAPHY

1. Abrahamsen, D. (1965). *The Road to Emotional Maturity*, New York: Prentice-Hall.
2. Alexander, F. and Staub, H. (1931). *The Criminal, the Judge and the Public*, Glencoe Free Press (1956).
3. Alexander, F. and Healy, W. (1935). *Roots of Crime: Psychoanalytic Studies*, Ann Arbor Microfilms, (1964).
4. American Psychiatric Association (1968), Publications Office, DSM-II. *Diagnostic and Statistical Manual of Mental Disorders*, Washington, D.C.
5. Baldwin, R. W. (1966). *Social Justice*, Oxford: Pergamon Press.
6. Baumhart, R. C. (1961). *How Ethical are Businessmen?* Harvard Business Review, 39, pp. 6-19, 156-176.
7. Bendheim, O. (1971). Personal Communication.
8. Bentham, J. (1789). *An Introduction to the Principles of Morals and Legislation*, Chapter III.
9. Berezin, M. A. and Cath, S. H. (1965). *Geriatric Psychiatry*, New York: International Universities Press.
10. Bergler, E. (1952). *The Superego*, New York: Grune and Stratton.
11. Bergler, E. and Meerloo, J. A. M. (1963). *Justice and Injustice*, New York: Grune and Stratton.
12. Busse, E. W. and Pfeiffer, E. (1969). (editors). *Behavior and Adaptation in Late Life*, Boston: Little, Brown.
13. Carnegie Foundation for the Advancement of Teaching (1956). See Heath, (1965) and Jahoda, (1958).
14. Comfort, A. (1964). *Ageing, the Biology of Senescence*, New York: Holt.
15. Critchley, M. (1953). *The Parietal Lobes*, New York: Stechert (1966).
16. Duffy, C. T. (1967). *Sex and Crime*, New York: Pocket Books.

17. Elkind, D. (1970). Erik Erikson's Eight Ages of Man, *New York Times Magazine*, April 12, 1970.
18. Engel, G. L. (1962). *Psychological Development in Health and Disease*, New York: Saunders.
19. Fenichel, O. (1945). *The Psychoanalytic Theory of Neurosis*, New York: Norton, p. 102.
20. Ferdinand, T. N. (1968). Sex Behavior and the American Class Structure: A Mosaic; *Annals of American Academy of Political and Social Science*, 376, pp. 76-85.
21. Ferenczi, S., see Fenichel, O. (1945).
22. Freedman, A. M. and Kaplan, H. I. (1967). *A Comprehensive Textbook of Psychiatry*, Baltimore: Williams and Wilkins.
23. Freud, A. (1946). *The Ego and the Mechanisms of Defense*, New York: International Universities Press.
24. Freud, S. (1900). *The Interpretation of Dreams*, Standard Edition; London: Hogarth.
25. Freud, S. (1905). *Three Essays on the Theory of Sexuality*, Standard Edition; London: Hogarth.
26. Freud, S. (1917). The Sense of Symptoms, (Lecture 17). *Introductory Lectures on Psychoanalysis*, Part III. Standard Edition; London: Hogarth.
27. Freud, S. (1923). *The Ego and the Id*, Standard Edition; London: Hogarth, p. 37.
28. Freud, S. (1926). *Psychoanalysis*, Standard Edition, vol. 20, p. 268; London: Hogarth.
29. Freud, S. (1927). *The Future of an Illusion*, Standard Edition; London: Hogarth, p. 11.
30. Freud, S. (1929). *Civilization and its Discontents*, Standard Edition; London: Hogarth, pp. 96, 102.
31. Giles, H. H. (1957). *Education and Human Motivation*, New York: Philosophical Library.
32. Ginsberg, M. (1965). *On Justice in Society*, Ithaca: Cornell University Press.
33. Goldstein, K. (1939). *The Organism*, New York: American Book Co.
34. Goldstein, K. (1942). *After-effects of Brain Injuries in War*, New York: Grune and Stratton.
35. Grinker, R. R. Sr., et al. (1962). Mentally Healthy Young Males (Homoclites), *Archives of Psychiatry*, 6 pp. 405-453.
36. Group for the Advancement of Psychiatry: Report #59, (1968).
37. Guze, S. B. and Cantwell, D. P. (1964). The Prognosis in Organic Brain Syndromes, *American Journal of Psychiatry*, 120 pp. 878-881.
38. Hart, H. L. A. (1968). *Punishment and Responsibility*, New York: Oxford University Press.
39. Hartmann, H. Kris E. and Loewenstein, R. (1949). Notes on the Theory of Aggression, *Psychoanalytic Study of the Child*, pp. 12-25.

40. Hartung, F. E. (1965). *Crime Law and Society*, Detroit: Wayne State University Press.
41. Heath, D. H. (1965). *Exploration of Maturity — Studies of Mature and Immature College Men*, New York: Appleton.
42. Henderson, D. and Gillespie, R. D. (1956). *A Textbook of Psychiatry*, London: Oxford University Press.
43. Hoffman, M. L. (1970). Moral Development, in Mussen, P. (editor) *Carmichael's Manual of Child Psychology*, New York: Wiley.
44. HSU (1962). See Heath (1965).
45. Jellinek, E. M. (1960). *The Disease Concept of Alcoholism*, New Haven: Hillhouse Press.
46. Jones, E. (1948). The Concept of a Normal Mind, *International Journal of Psychoanalysis*, 29, pp. 174-176.
47. Journal of the American Medical Association, Notes and Queries, Sept. 18, 1957.
48. Kastenbaum, R. (1965) (editor). *Contribution to the Psychology of Aging*, New York: Springer.
49. Katz, S., Goldstein, J. and Dershowitz, A. M. (1967). *Psychoanalysis, Psychiatry and Law*, New York: Free Press.
50. Kelsen, H. (1960). *What is Justice?* Berkeley: University of California Press.
51. Kinsey, A. C. et al. (1948). *Sexual Behavior in the Human Male*, Philadelphia: W. B. Saunders.
52. Kinsey, A. C. et al. (1953). *Sexual Behavior in the Human Female*, Philadelphia: W. B. Saunders.
53. Klein. See Offer (1968).
54. Kohlberg, L. (1964). Development of Moral Character and Moral Ideology in Hoffman, M. L. and Hoffman, L. W. *Review of Child Development Research*, vol. 1; New York: Russell Sage Foundation, pp. 383-432, p. 392.
55. Kubie, L. S. (1954). The Fundamental Nature of the Distinction between Normality and Neurosis, *Psychoanalytic Quarterly*, 23, pp. 167-204.
56. Ladd, J. (1964). Law and Morality: Internalism versus Externalism, in Hook, S. (editor) *Law and Philosophy*, New York: University Press.
57. Langner, T. S. and Michael, S. T. (1963). *Life Stress and Mental Health*, London: Free Press of Glencoe.
58. Lederer, W. (1964). Dragons, Delinquents and Destiny: An Essay on Positive Superego Functions, *Psychological Issues*, vol. 4, no. 3. Monograph 15, pp. 1-76.
59. McAllister, W. K. (1957). The Pleasure-Pain Principle in Bentham and Freud, *Archives of Criminal Psychodynamics*, 2, pp. 458-476.
60. Maccoby, E. E. (1968). The Development of Moral Values and Behavior in Childhood, in Clausen, J. A. (editor), *Socialization and Society*, Boston: Little, Brown.

61. MacDonald, J. M. (1969). *Psychiatry and the Criminal* Springfield, Illinois: C. C. Thomas.
62. Manis, M. (1971). *An Introduction to Cognitive Psychology*, Belmont (Calif.), Brooks: Cole, Publ.
63. Masters, W. H. and Johnson, V. E. (1966). *Human Sexual Response*, Boston: Little, Brown.
64. Masters, W. H. and Johnson V. E. (1970). *Human Sexual Inadequacy*, Boston: Little, Brown.
65. Menaker, E. and Menaker, W. (1965). *Ego in Evolution*, New York: Grove Press.
66. Menninger, (1950). See Grinker (1962).
67. Milgram, S. (1965). Conditions of Obedience and Disobedience to Authority, *Human Relations*, 18, pp. 57-76.
68. Morris, C. (1971). *The Justification of the Law*, Philadelphia: University of Pennsylvania Press.
69. Nemiah, J. C. (1967). See Freedman (1967).
70. Nixon, R. E. (1962). *The Art of Growing*, New York: Random House.
71. Noyes, A. P. and Kolb, L. C. (1963). *Modern Clinical Psychiatry*, Philadelphia, W. B. Saunders.
72. Nunberg, H. (1955). *Principles of Psychoanalysis*, New York: International Universities Press.
73. Offer, D. and Sabshin, M. (1968). *Normality: Theoretical and Clinical Concepts of Mental Health*, New York: Basic Books.
74. Pattison, E. M. (1968). Ego Morality: An Emerging Psychotherapeutic Concept, *Psychoanalytic Review*, Summer 1968, pp. 187-222.
75. Perelman, C. (1967). *Justice*, New York: Random House.
76. Piaget, J. (1932). *The Moral Development of the Child*, New York: Keegan, Paul.
77. Pound, R. (1951). *Justice According to Law*, New Haven: Yale University Press.
78. Pryce, (1970). The Normal Range *Journal of the American Medical Association* 212, p. 884.
79. Rainwater, L. (1966). The Crucible of Identity: The Negro Lower Class Family, *Daedalus* 95, pp. 172-216.
80. Rawls, J. (1964. Legal Obligation and the Duty of Fair Play in Hook, S. (editor) *Law and Philosophy*, New York: University Press.
81. Rawls, J. (1971). *A Theory of Justice*, Cambridge: Harvard University Press.
82. Roche, P. Q. (1967). *The Criminal Mind; A Study of Communication between Criminal Law and Psychiatry*, New York: Wiley.
83. Ruesch. See Wells (1945).
84. Sebald, H. (1968). *Adolescence; A Sociological Analysis*, New York: Appleton.
85. Srole, L. et al. (1962). *Mental Health in the Metropolis*, New York: McGraw-Hill.

86. Stieglitz, E. J. (1946). *The Second Forty Years*, Philadelphia: Lippincott.

87. Stone, J. (1965). *Human Law and Human Justice*, Stanford University Press.

88. Sutherland, A. E. (1956). *The Law and One Man among Many*, Madison: University of Wisconsin Press.

89. Sutherland, E. H. and Cressey, D. R. (1966). *Principles of Criminology*, Philadelphia: Lippincott.

90. Szasz, R. S. (1960). The Myth of Mental Illness, *American Psychologist*, 15, pp. 113-118.

91. Taber, M. (1969). et al. Disease Ideology and Mental Health Research, *Social Problems*, Winter 1969. pp. 349-357.

92. Tapp, J. L. (1969). Psychology and the Law, *Psychology Today*, vol. 2. pp. 16-22, (Feb. 1969).

93. Tapp, J. L. (1970). A Child's Garden of Law and Order, *Psychology Today*, vol. 4. p. 29, (Dec. 1970).

94. Tapp, J. L. (1971). Reflections, *Journal of Social Issues*, 27. vol. 2, pp. 1-16.

95. Tapp, J. L. and Kohlberg, L. (1971). Developing Senses of Law and Justice, *Journal of Social Issues*, 27. vol. 2, pp. 65-91.

96. Udry, J. R. (1968). Sex and Family Life, *Annals of American Academy of Political and Social Science*, 376. pp. 25-35.

97. Vital and Health Statistics: Data from the National Health Survey. National Center for Health Statistics, Series 10, Number 45, U.S. Dept. of Health, Education and Welfare Public Health Service.

98. Wells, F. L. and Ruesch, J. (1945). *Mental Examiners Handbook*, New York: Psychological Corporation.

99. Williams. See Offer (1958).

100. World Federation of Mental Health Commission (1945). See Heath, (1965).

101. Zinberg, N. E. and Kaufman, I. (1963). *Normal Psychology of the Aging Process*, New York: International Universities Press.

INDEX

CONTENTS

168

CONTENTS